Images of the South

Images of the South

*Constructing a Regional
Culture on Film and Video*

Karl G. Heider, Editor

Southern Anthropological Society Proceedings, No. 26
Mary W. Helms, Series Editor

The University of Georgia Press
Athens and London

Southern Anthropological Society
Founded 1966

OFFICERS, 1991–92

Thomas W. Collins, President
Alvin W. Wolfe, President-Elect
Daryl White, Secretary-Treasurer
Alice B. Kasakoff, Councilor
Benita J. Howell, Councilor
Gifford S. Nickerson, Councilor
Mary W. Helms, Series Editor
Gifford S. Nickerson, Newsletter Editor

Program Coordinator, 1991
Morgan Maclachlan

© 1993 by Southern Anthropological Society
All rights reserved
Published by the University of Georgia Press
Athens, Georgia 30602

Set in 11/13 Times Roman
The paper in this book meets the guidelines for
permanence and durability of the Committee on
Production Guidelines for Book Longevity of the
Council on Library Resources.

Printed in the United States of America

97 96 95 94 93   C   5 4 3 2 1

97 96 95 94 93   P   5 4 3 2 1

Library of Congress Cataloging in Publication Data
Images of the South : constructing a regional culture on film and video /
   Karl G. Heider, editor.
      p. cm. — (Southern Anthropological Society proceedings ; no. 26)
      Includes bibliographical references and index.
      ISBN 0-8203-1471-4 (alk. paper). — ISBN 0-8203-1472-2
(pbk. : alk. paper)
      1. Southern States in motion pictures. I. Heider, Karl G., 1935–
II. Series.
GN2.S9243 no.26
[PN1995.9.S66]
301 s—dc20
[791.43′6275]   92-6044

British Library Cataloging in Publication Data available

Contents

Introduction   1
Karl G. Heider

PART 1: Fictions from the Studios

Paradise Lost: Louisiana as a Microcosm of the South
in Fictional and Documentary Films   9
Ethelyn G. Orso

Religion and Representation in the Filmic South   24
Gary W. McDonogh and Cindy Hing-Yuk Wong

Scenes from a Dream: (Nearly) Lost Images of Black
Entertainers   55
Alex Albright

PART 2: Opportunities from the Archives

Ordinary Life in the Southern Appalachians, 1925–1940:
The Photographs of R. A. Romanes   77
Max E. White

Constructing the Florida Seminole on Film, 1850–1950   86
Patsy West

Moving Images of the Filmic South: Mining the WSB
Television Collection   103
John Edgar Reid, Jr.

Was It Not Real? Democratizing Myth Through
Ken Burns's *The Civil War*   112
James Peacock and Virginia Moore

PART 3: Statements from the People

Twixt the Holler and the Mall: Appalshop Films and the
Politics of Image in an Eastern Kentucky Classroom 127
Robert Gipe and Ann Messer

Bent, But Not Broken: Hurricane Hugo, Video, and
Community-Centered Learning 146
Gail Matthews

PART 4: On Snakes and People

"Bizarre Snake Handlers": Popular Media and a
Southern Stereotype 163
Jim Birckhead

The Worm and the Snake 190
Benjamin Dunlap

Contributors 201

Index 205

Images of the South

Introduction

Karl G. Heider

This volume considers a very contemporary anthropological problem: how have our versions of the South been constructed on film and videotape? A touch of fashionable reflexivity, a bit of visual anthropology.

Respectable historians could still in 1990 contribute to a book whose title asks the question, What made the South different? They responded with the traditional strategy of lining up historical facts as explanations. (The book was edited by Kees Gispen with contributions by George M. Fredrickson, Elizabeth Fox-Genovese, Eugene Genovese, and others.) Anthropologists are more likely to read the same question quite differently: not "what made the South different," but who told what sorts of stories; how did they put together their versions; which, of all the different possible pieces of the truth, did they choose; and why? The historians rearrange old facts, mix them with newly discovered or realized facts, and say something new. The anthropologists, as usual, stand back and try to explain what someone else is doing.

This volume is also visual anthropology. Although for years there has been a Society for Visual Anthropology as a constituent organization of the American Anthropological Association, it is still difficult to define "visual anthropology." Certainly it involves using film and video in various anthropological endeavors. Any definition of visual anthropology produces lists: different sorts of media (still photography, video, etc.), genres (ethnographic films, feature films, etc.), and anthropological goals (teaching, research, etc.). Even then, the lists always end with an "etc."

The papers in this volume provide an exemplary model of visual anthropology.[1] The different contributors examine a wide range of visual texts, asking how various people have used these visual media to construct their images of the South. These texts include still photographs, television news footage, students' videos, documentary, ethnographic and folkloric films, and unabashedly fictional feature films. Some texts were created by foreigners, others by natives or by scholars; they were motivated by sympathy, empathy, self-revelation, financial greed, and even prurience. Some derive from the middle of the last century, others were shown on national television last year.

All these contributors and texts, and more, came together for an exciting few days during the Key Symposium at the Southern Anthropological Society meeting in Columbia, South Carolina, in April 1991. The papers in this volume report what happened. But the printed word is a pale reflection of the speakers' dynamism, and a few still photographs can only hint at the variety of projected images that accompanied the papers.

I regret that, for one reason or another, some papers could not be included here, for they would have further expanded the scope of this volume. Leland Ferguson discussed Alex West's M.A. thesis film, *The Strength of Their Arms*, which concerns Ferguson's nineteenth-century African-American archaeological project on the South Carolina Low Country and what happened when BBC-TV hired West and remade his film for broadcast (a reconstruction of West's construction of Ferguson's construction via archaeological reconstruction). Mark Spagnolo, anthropologically trained and now a commercial filmmaker, described what happened to a film about Hurricane Hugo that he made for an electrical power co-operative which gave the film as Christmas and thank-you presents to its heroic linesmen who brought the region "back hot" in short time. (Spagnolo's cutting was recut.) Charles Joyner described "Gullah Tales," his television dramatization of African-American folktales, and Tom Whiteside told about H. Lee Waters, an itinerant filmmaker who roamed the small towns of the Carolinas in the 1930s shooting ordinary people in ordinary settings and then charging them admission to see themselves on screen. Beatriz Morales described how her anthropology students from Georgia State University collaborated with the Yoruba community in Atlanta to produce a mutually satisfactory account of Yoruba ritual.

In spite of these omissions, the range of this volume is broad and, in terms of approaches and methods, as diverse as possible. Some of the pieces are definitive and stand on their own. Others are provocative suggestions that illuminate barely explored parts of the overall spectrum.

The aim is to provide both solid meat and provocative flavor to many different tastes.

But it all spirals back to the South: not so much what it is, as how different people have constructed it. Of course, one is on shaky ground even speaking of "the South," which contains so many cultures. These pages include papers on the Appalachian South, the plantation South, the black urban South, Seminoles, the Civil War, and even a parody of it all. The book is really about Images of *Some* Souths, or Constructions of a Few Regional Subcultures, but that would be an impossible title. So it stands as *Images of the South*.

Fewer than half of the contributors to this volume are, strictly speaking, anthropologists. This fact demonstrates the eclectic nature of visual anthropology. Even a confirmed anthropologist like James Peacock, known for his studies of theater and religion in Indonesia and the South, here reaches beyond his usual beat to look at the television series *The Civil War*. Many old boundaries are falling in the 1990s. This two-way traffic across old frontiers is intellectually exhilarating, for we can see the birth of new ways of making connections. This volume does not bring visual anthropology in the South, or anywhere, to climax, but it should open many doors for anthropologists.

Part 1, "Fictions from the Studios," uses feature films as texts to examine how a culture is constructed when fiction and fantasy are unconstrained by any requirement for documentary veracity. Several anthropologists made serious attempts in this direction in the 1940s, initially to study enemy cultures during World War II (Bateson 1953; Benedict 1946; and Mead and Metraux 1953). This culminated, but for a time ended, with Wolfenstein and Leites's comparisons of cultural themes in American, English, and French films (1950). Only recently has this interest been revived with studies on Brazilian television (Kottak 1990), Japanese film (Ohnuki-Tierney 1990), and Indonesian cinema (Heider 1991). In this section, we have Ethelyn Orso's analysis of a parody, *Fletch Lives*. Although we begin with parody, it is in fact the last word, for parody is only possible after the pattern has been so firmly established—so definitively constructed—that it can be manipulated in fun. Gary W. McDonogh and Cindy Hing-Yuk Wong use *Nashville, Sergeant York*, and other films to look specifically at images of religion. And Alex Albright puts the early black ensemble musical *Pitch a Boogie Woogie* into its cultural context.

Part 2, "Opportunities from the Archives," includes Max White's examination of still photographs made by an expatriate German who lived in the southern Appalachians. Patsy West follows many photographers who over a hundred years produced various images of the Seminoles. While anthropologists have often examined still photographs (see, for example, Scherer 1990), John Edgar Reid's contribution on the archives of an Atlanta television station opens an entirely untouched treasure trove of visual data. By implication, Reid's is the single most challenging paper. While the other papers go far to show what emerges when anthropologists look at visual records, Reid says here it is, use it if you have the wit. Ken Burns's *The Civil War* comprised hundreds of century-old still photographs molded into a story. James Peacock and Virginia Moore discuss how that particular version "democratizes the myth."

Part 3, "Statements from the People," begins with Robert Gipe and Ann Messer writing about Appalshop, that influential center of activity, film, and otherwise, as it deals with its own culture of Appalachia. Gail Matthews, a folklorist, relates how she provided video cameras to South Carolina school children still traumatized by Hurricane Hugo and how they constructed their own stories. While anthropology began as accounts of cultures by outsiders, in recent years it has been more sensitive to, and more supportive of, the voices of the people themselves. Yet, somehow, these voices are often challenged in print and at conferences from a hyperpositivistic position. Outsiders, whose objectivity is simply taken for granted, challenge the reliability of the natives! The positivist assumption that there is objective truth out there is a vexing problem for anthropology, and the same person can be found arguing both sides of the question without contradiction (Heider 1983 *vs.* Heider 1988). Jane Gaines, in her criticism of the Appalshop approach (1989) raised the more subtle problem of whether these films, whoever makes them, should preserve culture or should show the context of the changing world. The three contributions in this section implicitly deal with both problems as they explicitly offer different models for listening to people's voices.

Part 4, "On Snakes and People," deals with one of the most exotic—no, we must say "exotically constructed"—cultural patterns of the twentieth-century South, the Pentacostal handling of serpents. Jim Birckhead tells how the media's prurient fascination with snake handling works against his attempts as an anthropologist to explain his Pentacostal friends. Similarly, Benjamin Dunlap tells the story of his hapless adventures trying to make sense of the mountain snake handlers to some people of the South Carolina coast. In the end we do not know whether to weep or to laugh, and if to laugh, at whom.

Now I, as editor of the volume, sit back and watch where each of these paths will take us over the next decade. It is an exciting prospect indeed.

NOTE

1. There have been isolated articles of this sort in earlier SAS volumes and elsewhere. See, for example, Nash 1987; Lewis 1990; and Roseman 1991.

REFERENCES

BATESON, GREGORY, 1953. An Analysis of the Film *Hitlerjunge Quex*. In Mead and Metraux, eds., *The Study of Culture at a Distance*, pp. 302–14.

BENEDICT, RUTH, 1946. *The Chrysanthemum and the Sword: Patterns of Japanese Culture* (Boston: Houghton Mifflin).

GAINES, JANE M., 1989. Appalshop Documentaries: Inventing and Preserving Appalachia. *Jump Cut* 43:53–62.

GISPEN, KEES, 1990. *What Made the South Different?* (Jackson: University Press of Mississippi).

HEIDER, KARL G., 1983. Fieldwork with a Camera. *Studies in Visual Communication* 9:2–10.

———, 1988. The Rashomon Effect: When Ethnographers Disagree. *American Anthropologist* 90:73–81.

———, 1991. *Indonesian Cinema. National Culture on Screen* (Honolulu: University of Hawaii Press).

KOTTAK, CONRAD PHILLIP, 1990. *Prime-Time Society: An Anthropological Analysis of Television and Culture* (Belmont, Calif.: Wadsworth).

LEWIS, HELEN M., 1990. Appalshop: Preserving, Participating in, and Creating Southern Mountain Culture. In *Cultural Heritage Conservation in the American South*, Benita J. Howell, ed. SAS Proceedings, no. 23 (Athens: University of Georgia Press), pp. 79–86.

MEAD, MARGARET, and RHODA METRAUX, 1953. *The Study of Culture at a Distance* (Chicago: University of Chicago Press).

NASH, JESSE, 1989. Icons of Sensuality and Childishness: Women in New

Orleans Advertising. In *Women in the South: An Anthropological Perspective*, Holly S. Mathews, ed. SAS Proceedings, no. 22 (Athens: University of Georgia Press), pp. 18–26.

OHNUKI-TIERNEY, EMIKO, 1990. The Ambivalent Self of the Contemporary Japanese. *Cultural Anthropology* 5:197–216.

ROSEMAN, SHARON R., 1991. A Documentary Fiction and Ethnographic Production: An Analysis of *Sherman's March*. *Cultural Anthropology* 6:505–24.

SCHERER, JOANNA COHAN, ed., 1990. Picturing Cultures: Historical Photographs in Anthropological Inquiry. Special issue of *Visual Anthropology* 3, parts 2–3.

WOLFENSTEIN, MARTHA, and NATHAN LEITES, 1950. *Movies: A Psychological Study* (Glencoe, Ill.: Free Press).

PART 1
Fictions from the Studios

Paradise Lost: Louisiana as a Microcosm of the South in Fictional and Documentary Films

Ethelyn G. Orso

The Bayou State, the Pelican State, Sportsman's Paradise: all have been used as special names for Louisiana, home of the first motion picture theater in the United States. In 1896, two entrepreneurs opened Vitascope Hall on the corner of Canal Street and Exchange Place in the heart of New Orleans. According to Don Lee Keith, it was love at first sight. Keith, who a hundred years later organized an exhibit at the Louisiana State Museum in New Orleans entitled "Starring Louisiana: A Romance of the Real and the Reel," says that by the end of 1896 "Louisiana's love affair with the movies had begun. Ever since then the feeling has been mutual for moviemakers. From the time of the silent era, producers have been captivated by Louisiana's charm and mystique" (Keith 1987:1). As a result, Louisiana became a very popular state for on-location shooting of fictional films about the South in general, and its scenery and people became familiar to American moviegoers across the nation. Photographs of specific Louisiana landmarks like Oak Alley Plantation near Vacherie are used regularly in films and elsewhere as visual cues for the Old South. Scores of commercial films were shot on location in Louisiana from the first, *Mephisto and the Maiden* in 1909, to the 1990 filming of Kate Chopin's *The Awakening*, starring Kelly McGillis.

Over time, Louisiana's love affair with the movies has come to be expressed in specific movie genres. Moviegoers in other regions of the nation have come to associate the themes in these genres simultaneously with the Pelican State and with the South in general, resulting in a mutual, palimpsest-like image.

Drama plays especially well in Louisiana. Whether the conflict concerns a romance gone sour, characters gone crazy, or politics gone awry, the struggle is enhanced when protagonist and antagonist slug it out amid ancient moss-draped live oaks or decaying plantation manors with colorful characters. Examples of this type of film shot in Louisiana include *All the King's Men*; *A Streetcar Named Desire*; *Walk on the Wild Side*; *The Long, Hot Summer*; *The Sound and the Fury*; *Panic in the Streets*; *Tarnished Angels*; *A Soldier's Story*; *Hard Times*; *Hotel*; *Sounder*; *Easy Rider*; and *Sex, Lies, and Videotape*.

Films focusing on crime, detectives, and police have also had wide box office appeal. Included in this category are *Cry of the Hunted*; *The Docks of New Orleans*; *Down by Law*; *The Drowning Pool*; *New Orleans Uncensored*; *Nightmare*; *This Woman Is Dangerous*; *Johnny Angel*; *Tightrope*; and *Fear Is the Key*.

Tennessee Williams once said that "Down in Louisiana they know that spooks are real." In commercial films, ghosts, ghouls, swamp monsters, cat people, and the like are just another dimension of life in Louisiana and the South in general. In a genre of films that Keith calls "Creepy Times Down South," one finds *The Alligator People*; *Cat People*; *The Creature from Black Lake*; *The Cry of the Werewolf*; *Hush, Hush Sweet Charlotte*; *Nightmare Honeymoon*; and *The Screams of a Winter Night*.

Since past and present coexist so peacefully in Louisiana and many other southern states, a genre Keith calls "It Themes Like Old Times" focuses on our graceful old plantations, old traditions, and the mighty Mississippi River. Film examples include *Band of Angels*; *The Beguiled*; *The Foxes of Harrow*; *Mandingo*; *The Mississippi Gambler*; and *My Forbidden Past*.

Some of the films made on location in the Pelican State emphasize unique elements such as music. Louisiana gave birth to the blues, a fact reinforced by several Hollywood films that featured native son Louis "Satchmo" Armstrong. The "King" (as in Creole), Elvis Presley also made two New Orleans–based smashes. Other musicals made in Louisiana include *The Birth of the Blues*; *Mardi Gras*; *Glory Alley*; *Rainbow on the River*; *Dixie*; *Louisiana Purchase*; *Mississippi*; *Sunny*; *Naughty Marietta*; *New Orleans*; and *The Toast of New Orleans*. Then there are the dozens of films in which Louisiana culture itself is the subject of the camera's lens, such films as *Belizaire the Cajun*; *Bourbon Street Shadows*; *The Buccaneer*; *Dixiana*; *Evangeline*; *Jezebel*; *The Lady from*

Louisiana; *Louisiana*; *The Louisiana Story*; *Pretty Baby*; *Thunder Bay*; *Alvarez Kelly*; *Angel Heart*; *Band of Angels*; *The Beguiled*; *Belle of the Nineties*; *The Big Easy*; *The Drowning Pool*; *French Quarter*; *Hurry Sundown*; *King Creole*; *The Lone Wolf*; *Mandingo*; *Nevada Smith*; *New Orleans*; *Sister, Sister*; *Southern Comfort*; *Streetcar Named Desire*; and *An Unwilling Hero*.

Given the extremely large number of fictional films shot on location in Louisiana during the past eighty years, the average American moviegoer has become visually saturated with Louisiana's landmarks, people, and culture. For the outsider then, the Bayou State has become the epitome of the old South. This is especially true for commercial Hollywood filmmakers, who frequently make that equation. A good example of the equation is found in the film comedy *Fletch Lives*. Shot on location in southern Louisiana, it was released by Universal Studios in 1989. Subsequently the film was aired twice by CBS during prime time: on Tuesday, December 18, 1990, and again on Saturday, May 4, 1991. Presumably, countless millions of persons have viewed it.

Generally reserving the state for more serious matters, Hollywood has made very few comedies on location in Louisiana, only three in the past twenty years: *Last of the Mobile Hot Shots*, *Let's Do It Again*, and *The Toy*. On the surface, *Fletch Lives* offers a humorous parody of corruption and crime in Louisiana politics, religion, and environmental policies. It also pokes fun at folks who are portrayed as having weak mentalities and moralities but strong southern accents. Because the film's title makes no mention of the South, or Louisiana, the unsuspecting moviegoer is at first caught off guard, expecting to be entertained by a slapstick sequel to Chevy Chase's earlier movie *Fletch* that was filmed in the western United States. Instead, the viewer observes the bashing of Louisiana with cheap shots and the vulgar form of comedy that Chase became associated with in his *Vacation* movie series.

Fletch Lives could have been filmed anywhere south of the Mason-Dixon line since the real target was not Louisiana but the entire "decadent" South. Louisiana was chosen because it already was a familiar cinematographic symbol for the South in general, well known to audiences around the United States and the world.

The Fletch films are based on characters created by detective book writer Gregory McDonald, but the screenplay for *Fletch Lives* was written by Leon Capetanos. Chevy Chase stars as Irwin Fletcher, nicknamed

"Fletch," a California detective-journalist who writes for a large Los Angeles newspaper under the pen name of Jane Doe. Harassed for alimony by his ex-wife's attorney and denied a long-awaited vacation, he learns that he has inherited a plantation in Thibodaux, Louisiana. He quits his job and travels to Louisiana to claim Belle Isle and to live the life of a rich southern plantation owner. *Fletch Lives* is also about a white American trickster-hero's desire to be black, his search for paradise in the South, and his subsequent discovery of a paradise lost, corrupted, and defiled.

In his essay "Film Images," Maurice Yacowar (1989:925–26) argues that "Hollywood has presented the South as a corrupted Eden, dwelling first on an idyllic image and later on a harsher 'realistic' vision. Throughout, the treatment of the South centers upon the tension between a mythic ideal and a severely flawed reality." Yacowar speaks of a "national myth" in connection with the depiction of the South, presumably suggesting that as the South was corrupted so was the rest of the nation. He states that as "America sees itself in both the mythic and the realistic depictions of the South, something of an unarticulated guilt often emerges through these chronicles of lost innocence."

Robert Flaherty, the "father of the documentary film," made his last film in 1948 in southern Louisiana and also touched upon the national myth of an original Eden of abundance and opportunity. In *Louisiana Story*, Flaherty concluded his career with a film containing "sparkling photography, scored, lyrical renditions of Cajun folk music, and a Hollywood 'happy-ever-after' ending." As Nicholas Spitzer (1985:215) observes, although the film's "style has stood up well, its content is less durable. The impact of the oil industry on Cajun society for good and ill is obviously more complex than the plot of . . . [the film]." Andrew Horton (1990) reached a similar conclusion in his essay "Beyond *Louisiana Story*." The plot of *Louisiana Story* can be summarized as follows: Cajuns live happily in the swamp, hunting and fishing; oil company barge comes and creates havoc by drilling and causing explosions; after disrupting paradise, oil company's exploration appears doomed to failure; Cajun boy resorts to traditional magic to reverse the fortunes of the high technology; oil is successfully pumped and the well is capped; the company leaves and the Cajun family lives happily ever after on the oil lease dividends.

Many years passed before another high quality film documentation of Louisiana traditional culture appeared. Florida-born but Tulane-educated filmmaker Les Blank began to document the Pelican State's culture in the late sixties with his romantic but affectionate portraits of Cajun and Creole life in southern Louisiana in films such as *Spend It All* (1970), and *Always for Pleasure* (1978). Blank, who was one of the cameramen for the 1969 film *Easy Rider* that was shot on location in New Orleans and southern Louisiana, has been criticized by Cajuns and scholars alike as being too shallow and a part of a Hollywood film-making style. Cajun folklorist Barry Ancelet (1987:886) says that films like those by Blank are "done by young Americans who seemed to be seeking a sort of 'paradise lost' and thought to have found it in French-Louisiana."

The search by young Americans for a paradise lost in the South (as in Louisiana) was a key element of the plot of the previously mentioned *Easy Rider* that starred Peter Fonda, Dennis Hopper, and Jack Nicholson. Horace Greeley's injunction "Go west, young man" helped convince millions seeking gold and the promised land to go to California in the middle of the nineteenth century. *Easy Rider* is the story of a group of young, twentieth-century, drug-using Californians who in a reverse trend ride their motorcycles eastward in search of the promised land. Their ride is ended in Louisiana, when, after attending the Mardi Gras and "dropping" LSD in an old New Orleans cemetery, their minds are literally "blown away" by a shotgun blast from a truckload of rednecks on a rural Louisiana highway. Hence, the Californian-American dream of rediscovering a paradise in the South is brutally ended in *Easy Rider*. Twenty years after *Easy Rider*, another unhappy California character named "Fletch" travels eastward to Louisiana to claim a piece of paradise, finding instead a "seriously flawed reality," a paradise lost. Being a comedy, however, *Fletch Lives* has a happy ending.

In perhaps the most significant scene in the film, Fletch has a dream while travelling by plane to Thibodaux, Louisiana, and Belle Isle, the "eighty acres of old plantation property" that he has inherited. The dream reveals both his great expectations and his equation of Belle Isle with a heavenly paradise.

The dream sequence opens with the camera passing through the almost pearly gates of a magnificent southern plantation mansion, in reality the Houmas House, located on the Mississippi River Road above New Orleans. An old southern black spiritual hymn is being sung that also suggests an entry to Heaven: "We are coming, we are coming, but our heads are bending low. Can you hear our gentle voices calling?" Significantly, at this point the lyrics have been changed from "Old Black Joe" to "Old *White* Joe." We soon realize that in addition to all the characters in the dream sequence wearing white clothing, they are all Caucasians! In other words, in Fletch's dream plantation in the South, there are no blacks. While on the surface this appears to be racist, since it would be the ideal heaven for white bigots, there is on another level a more likely interpretation.

In his dream, Fletch is seated on the veranda of a stately Louisiana plantation mansion with Betty Lee, a buxom and beautiful Scarlett O'Hara type at his side. He is called "Colonel" and is waited upon by servants played by his ex-wife's attorney and his former boss. He declines an offer to be entertained by the field hands and instead breaks into his own rendition of "Zip-a-dee Doo-Dah" to which all the white plantation folk begin dancing and singing with unmitigated joy.

The scenes in Fletch's dream are parodic recreations of the 1948 Walt Disney cartoon film *Song of the South*, which was rereleased during the 1980s. The film is based on Joel Chandler Harris's Georgia collections of black southern folktales and features a black Uncle Remus who tells white children stories of the trickster Brer Rabbit.

Interpretations by Roger Abrahams (1970) of the Brer Rabbit folktale cycle indicate that the stories have an obvious relationship to social relations between blacks and whites before the Civil War. The trickster tales can be seen as a veiled reaction or protest against white domination, and as a way of presenting feelings of protest in a nonthreatening way. For blacks in the United States, the trickster represents the hero who can be in control of his world only through cleverness. The humor of these tales serves to release tension in a situation in which open rebellion seems futile.

Children watching the Disney film are perhaps unaware that Brer Rabbit symbolizes a black trickster trying to outwit the whites around him. The audience watching *Fletch Lives* is likewise unaware that the film will show Fletch reenacting the kinds of wily deeds and daring escapes used by Brer Rabbit, a black trickster-hero in disguise.

The only black character in the Fletch film is Calculus Zanzibee, a genuine black trickster. Calculus says that his great-grandfather was "owned by Fletch's great-grandfather." He plays the stereotypical part of a Step-and-Fetch-It type house servant who lives in a shack at Belle Isle. While appearing to be slow and stupid, he cons Fletch and the other whites into doing their own work. Calculus, the genuine black trickster, and Fletch, the pseudoblack trickster, work together to outwit their adversaries in several humorous episodes. At the end of the film it is revealed that Calculus is not really a southern black, as his stereotypical behavior would suggest, but rather an undercover FBI agent named Goldstein, suggesting that his true ethnic identity is Jewish.

The lead character in *Fletch Lives* is a white trickster hero who has a secret wish to be black. In the earlier film, *Fletch*, the lead character has a dream in which he is a Los Angeles Laker basketball player wearing dark makeup and an Afro wig. In *Fletch Lives*, he uses the name "Eldridge Cleaver" when he impersonates a corpse at the morgue. Later, when he crashes a Civil War costume party, he claims to be "Bobby Lee Schwartz" (black). This interpretation is further supported by Fletch's perpetual adulation of the Los Angeles Lakers basketball team, depicted as cool black dudes who are heroes of the courts. Fletch has photographs of Laker players and other Laker paraphernalia on the walls of his apartment and office. He wears a Laker cap and Laker high-tops, and whenever time permits, he shoots hoops. In a dialogue on the airplane prior to his dream sequence, Fletch tells a woman that he is wearing a Laker championship watch because it is all he has to remember from the Laker that he used to date. In this light, then, Fletch's dream of the all-white plantation is not necessarily racist. He wants to be like Brer Rabbit, a disguised black trickster-hero, but he wants to be the *only* such black character in heaven.

After the dream sequence, Fletch arrives in Thibodaux where he has to face the kind of "severely flawed reality" that Yacowar described. Belle Isle, the heavenly plantation of his dream, is not only a paradise lost but is also polluted with toxic wastes. Louisiana, he learns, is inhabited by a host of villains and disreputable characters: a deceitful televangelist named Farnsworth who owns a Bible Land theme park, Heavenly Hilton Hotel and Convention Center, and Bible College; Loyal Sons of the White Race who burn down his house; and murderous and corrupt lawyers and policemen. None of these obstacles is sufficient, however, to overcome the trickster's abilities to succeed and attain a happy Hollywood ending. After successfully employing several disguises and cleverly outwitting all the exceedingly stupid southerners who are after his inheritance, Fletch decides to return to California with Becky Ann, the televangelist's daughter whom he has seduced. Prior to their departure for Los Angeles, he tells her, "You need to get away from this chemical swamp! Do you like smog?"

Back in Los Angeles, Fletch is given a surprise party by his coworkers at the newspaper and learns that he has been awarded $100,000 in fire insurance money for the manor house that was destroyed at Belle Isle. Then his ex-wife's lawyer shows up and lays claim to half of the recently inherited Louisiana property. In an apparently generous move, Fletch signs all of Belle Isle over to her (knowing that it is a toxic waste dump site) with the agreement that she forego any other claims upon him. As he signs the papers relinquishing his rights to the property, he says to the attorney, "Does it please you to rip out my ancestral roots? I was born and raised in a briar patch." The duped attorney does not make the obvious connection between the "briar patch" and the story of Brer Rabbit's escape from the Tar Baby. The movie ends with loud Zydeco music and the understanding that Fletch is indeed a successful trickster, a Brer Rabbit character reincarnated. Not only has he escaped permanently from his ex-wife's claims and her attorney, the Southern crooks who wanted to rob and kill him, *and* the sticky tar on his land, but he gets a promotion and private office back at the Los Angeles newspaper, and he can keep the $100,000 insurance refund and the southern girlfriend, Becky Ann, if so inclined.

Fletch Lives presents a biased and negative view of the South in general, and not just Louisiana. It uses many of the tired old stereotypes of southerners and southern culture that have been around for at least a century, stereotypes that may be thought of as folklore. Folklore acts to reinforce group identity as well as divide people in terms of molding or confirming one group's attitudes about another group. The folklorist William Hugh Jansen (1965:43) has observed that nearly every nation has a city or region that is the target for *intra*group ethnic slurs. In Greece it is the island of Chios; in Mexico, the city of Monterrey. In France it is Pontoise; in Colombia, the town of Pasto. In the United States, it is the South. These ethnic slur traditions have an important effect in the formation of deep-seated prejudices. Consequently, films like *Fletch Lives* not only reflect negative stereotypes of the South and southerners, but they also help to reinforce and perpetuate them by engendering them in young viewers.

The various elements of the southern stereotype portrayed in *Fletch Lives* will now be considered. It might be noted that they are especially invalid for southern Louisiana where the movie was filmed since its culture is derived from southern European (French and Spanish) Catholic roots. Southern Louisiana, with its transplanted Mediterranean-Catholic elements, is unlike other areas of the deep South with their Anglo-Saxon Protestant antecedents.

SOUTHERN SPEECH

The Southern Drawl

Among the several geographical regions of the continental United States, the South is the one area consistently depicted as having unique speech habits. In fictional films, southerners are portrayed as Americans with strong regional accents. In films about the South, actors and actresses who are not from the South are expected to duplicate the southern drawl, often with disastrous consequences.

The plantation chosen to be "Belle Isle" is Belle Helene, located in Geismer, in southern Louisiana. The native people of southern Louisiana and Thibodaux, where *Fletch Lives* was filmed, have nothing resembling a southern drawl. Thibodaux lies in the heart of French Acadian country where the local accent derives from Acadian French. Regardless of that, all of the Louisiana characters in the film speak like folks from *north* Louisiana, Mississippi, or even Georgia, with thick southern accents.

The Southern Vocabulary

In concert with their drawls, southerners are consistently typecast as persons having quaint and picturesque vocabularies and who habitually use words that derive from the Civil War. For example: Y'all; Y'all come; Yankee (or Damnyankee—one word); carpetbagger.

Accused of Amanda Ray's murder, Fletch is framed and jailed. The corrupt lawyer who gets Fletch out on bail says he is ashamed that "things like this go on in the *New* South" and that twenty years ago "Yankees" like Fletch used to be killed. People in southern Louisiana do not call their part of the world the "new South," nor do they refer to outsiders as "Yankees." At another point in the film, Fletch is called a "carpetbagger."

Flowery Southern Phrasing

Films portray southerners with odd vocabularies and a strong drawl, and also with flowery and poetic speech habits. Hamilton Johnson, the lawyer who gets Fletch out of jail, is a master of such language, and tells Fletch while driving, "Just smell that soft, southern air!" A minute later, they drive past an oil refinery that is berated by the lawyer for spoiling the smell.

Southern Names

Although "Bubba" is often used in films for a character playing a stupid Southern male, there is no Bubba in *Fletch Lives*. However, all the women in the film have names like Cindy May, Betty Lee, Lottie Pearl, Becky Ann, and Amanda Ray. Although such names are not typical for girls in southern Louisiana, they are consistent with the widespread perception elsewhere in the United States that there is a southern naming custom of giving girls two first names.

In *Fletch Lives*, practically everyone has two first names. Men are named Billy Bob, Jimmy Lee, or Billy Ray. While in jail, Fletch misunderstands the name of his cellmate as "Ben Dover," and comments that he is the only person who doesn't have a middle name.

SOUTHERN WOMEN AS SEX-HUNGRY FEMALES

From Scarlett O'Hara to Tennessee Williams's character Maggie the Cat to the *Golden Girls*'s Blanche Devereaux, southern women are frequently typecast as females with large sexual appetites that never seem to be satisfied.

In the dream sequence of *Fletch Lives*, the buxom Betty Lee asks Fletch if he minds if she sits on his lap. Such behavior typifies the aggressive sexuality southern women are supposed to display. Amanda

Ray, the attorney who meets Fletch at the Thibodaux airport, later takes him to her elegant home for dinner. When he says he'll take things "slow and easy" (referring to his decision about his land), she offers herself for dessert, "something sweet and southern." The next scene shows them together in her bed. Finally there is Becky Ann, the televangelist's young daughter, who becomes Fletch's last sexual partner. In contrast to the aggressive sexuality of the two other (older) women, she is just easy to seduce.

Frequently the oversexed southern woman is given an appropriate name such as Scarlett (as in *The Scarlet Letter*) O'Hara, or a French name such as Blanche Devereaux. The latter practice results in a combined ethnic slur stereotype, since the French woman already had a reputation that preceded the southern version.

THE SOUTH AS THE CENTER OF RACISM

The South may be the birthplace of the Ku Klux Klan, but currently racism is more overt and volatile in other regions of the United States such as the West. For example, there are several powerful white supremacy groups headquartered in the West, yet the South continues to be targeted for blame when it comes to racism.

In *Fletch Lives*, a group of men wearing white sheets in the style of the Ku Klux Klan makes an appearance at Belle Isle. Their leader, the "Grand Klegle," has organized his "Loyal Sons of the White Race" to chant "Scum, scum, scum! Go back to where you're from!" Then they burn crosses on Fletch's lawn. The "Grand Klegle" explains to his men that Fletch is a "Carpetbagger," certainly not a commonly used label in southern Louisiana for newcomers from California.

SOUTHERN HOSPITALITY

Southerners often take pride in their friendliness and hospitality, another example of their esoteric folklore. But the film shows that outsiders often take a negative, exoteric view of what the "hospitality" includes. For example, Fletch has dinner in a small cafe in Thibodaux where he is consoled for all the bad luck he has had, including the loss of the house at Belle Isle due to arson. As compensation, he is offered some "genuine southern hospitality."

The southern hospitality turns out to be an invitation to join a group of drunken men for a coon hunt late at night in the woods. The men wear flashlights on their hats, drink moonshine from a mason jar, and let the hounds do the work of treeing the raccoon. At one point during the hunt, Fletch becomes the target for an unknown assassin. In southern Louisiana, duck hunting is a typical all-male bonding activity, not coon hunting. Probably only people in Hollywood would consider a coon hunt to be an example of southern Louisiana or southern hospitality.

SOUTHERNERS AS LAWLESS AND WILD

This element of the stereotype derives directly from the secession of the southern states from the Union and the subsequent Civil War. In his 1943 book *The Fighting South*, John Temple Graves noted that in every American war southerners have joined up to fight in larger numbers than residents of other regions, in part due to a streak of daring in the southern character that has been noted by many writers (Wardlaw 1991:B-7).

Television's "The Dukes of Hazard" epitomized a modern-day stereotype of young, twentieth-century southern rebels. *Smokey and the Bandit* and other Hollywood films also employ the motif of the lawless southerner behind the wheel of a fast car.

In one scene of *Fletch Lives*, Fletch enters a roadside tavern in Thibodaux that is filled with leather-clad motorcyclists, members of an outlaw gang called the "Nazis from Natchez."

THE ENDLESS EMPHASIS ON THE CIVIL WAR

At a southern mansion, Fletch crashes a formal party given by Hamilton Johnson, the eloquent but corrupt lawyer, for members of the Pontchartrain Society, a group of Louisiana conservationists. The men are wearing Confederate military attire or Civil War period outfits while the women are in hoop-skirted gowns. Although not typical Louisiana costume party clothing of 1989, such outfits are suitable attire for southerners who, the stereotype claims, can never forget "the War."

THE STUPID SOUTHERNER

One of the most insidious elements of the stereotype concerns the intelligence of southern folk which consistently is depicted as being lower than elsewhere in the United States. Indeed, stupidity appears to be one element in common in all intragroup ethnic slurs.

The first southerner Fletch meets is a dumb blonde named Cindy May who is seated next to him on the plane as he travels to Thibodaux. She went all the way to California for a nose job and is returning to Selma (Alabama) with bruises and bandages on her face. She is a nuisance and a bonehead and misunderstands Fletch's alias of "Nostradamus" as "Notre Dame," the university.

Calculus Zanzibee, the only black character in the film, is also shown as slow and dimwitted. His character reflects the essence of the stereotype of the ignorant southern black who has not even "heard of the Emancipation Proclamation." Some of his lines seem to be parodic reinforcements of racial stereotypes, as when he says that he is only happy when he's working (for whites). Although we learn at the end of the film that he is an undercover FBI agent, up until that point we are presented with a barrage of negative stereotypes concerning black southerners.

Sometimes the emphasis is on simple southern naivete as shown in the widespread popular acceptance of fraudulent religious practitioners such as Jim and Tammy Bakker, or Jimmy Swaggart. *Fletch Lives* makes extensive use of this stereotype and shows how a fictitious televangelist, the Reverend Jimmy Lee Farnsworth, uses trickery and deception to impress his gullible southern audience. Another part of the plot of *Fletch Lives* invokes this pose of naivete when we learn that the mother of the corrupt attorney, Hamilton Johnson, was duped into signing over all her assets to Farnsworth, as was Fletch's aunt until she changed her will just before she died.

Fletch frequently capitalizes, in a slapstick manner, on the general ignorance of the stereotypical southerner. For example, in one scene he convinces a policeman that a "cannibal termite" has fallen into his ear. Fletch convinces the cop that to remove it he must drop to the floor, slap his head, and squeal like a pig!

STRANGE SOUTHERN EATING HABITS

In one scene, Fletch and Calculus eat dinner in a greasy-spoon type cafe. Fletch's fried catfish is served with the whiskers and head still attached, prompting him to ask if they serve everything that way. When the waitress says "yes," he retorts that he's glad he didn't order a hamburger! In an earlier scene, Fletch jokes about "chitlins," which he thinks are furry little animals.

Southerners are frequently stereotyped as having unorthodox food preferences for things like sow belly, hog jowls, chitlins, hush puppies, corn pone, grits, moonshine, and mint juleps. But then such odd foods would be expected from unintelligent people with two first names who speak with a drawl, are lawless and wild racists, and who can never forget the Civil War!

Maurice Yacowar (1989:925–26) said that the United States saw itself in both the mythic and the realistic depictions of the South and that an unarticulated guilt emerges through these chronicles of lost innocence. *Fletch Lives* is also about the paradise that was America (and not just Louisiana or the South) that has been lost, despoiled, and destroyed by corruption, stupidity, and greed. Love Canal is not located in Louisiana, nor does the state have the radioactive wastes associated with nuclear arms factories in other parts of the nation. Rachel Carson's "Silent Spring" flowed first in the Northeast. Political corruption is not unique to Louisiana or even the South for that matter. Recent scandals have mainly affected loan institutions in the West, that place of opportunity where young Americans were advised to go in the last century. In other words, "When America sees itself in Hollywood's South, the flawed present harkens back to another Eden, fragile and spent. Hollywood's South stands as one of the nation's key cultural myths" (Yacowar 1989:927).

NOTE

The editor of this volume suggested that production stills from *Fletch Lives* be used to illustrate this essay. Unfortunately, the monetary costs of obtaining permissions and the legal necessity of obtaining the consent of all persons portrayed in the stills exceeded practical limits.

REFERENCES

ABRAHAMS, ROGER D., 1970. *Deep Down in the Jungle* (Chicago: Aldine).
ANCELET, BARRY, 1978. *Le Son des Cajuns*. Film review in *Journal of American Folklore* 91:885–86.
GRAVES, JOHN TEMPLE, 1943. *The Fighting South* (New York: Putnam's Sons).
HORTON, ANDREW, 1990. Beyond *Louisiana Story*: Less Art and More Truth for Independent Documentary Film-makers in Louisiana. *Cultural Vistas* (Winter): 4–8. Published by the Louisiana Endowment for the Humanities.
JANSEN, WILLIAM HUGH, 1965. The Esoteric-Exoteric Factor in Folklore. In *The Study of Folklore*, Alan Dundes, ed. (Englewood Cliffs, N.J.: Prentice-Hall), pp. 43–51.
KATZ, ALLAN, 1990. The Bureaucracy of Film-Making. *New Orleans Magazine* 24(11): 29.
KEITH, DON LEE, 1987. Starring Louisiana: A Romance of the Real and the Reel (New Orleans: Louisiana State Museum Program).
———, 1990. A Place Called New Orleans and a Thing Called Music. *New Orleans Magazine* 24(11): 28.
KRAUSS, DAVID, 1990. Hollywood's New Orleans. *New Orleans Magazine* 24(11): 21–30.
SPITZER, NICHOLAS, 1985. An Introduction to Media Documentation of Louisiana Folklife. In *Louisiana Folklife: A Guide to the State*, N. Spitzer, ed. (Baton Rouge: Louisiana Folklife Program), pp. 200–20.
WARDLAW, JACK, 1991. South Usually Bears Larger Share of Military Burden. *Times-Picayune*, Sunday, January 20, Sec. B, p. 7.
YACOWAR, MAURICE, 1989. Film Images. In *Encyclopedia of Southern Culture*, Charles R. Wilson and William Ferris, eds. (Chapel Hill: University of North Carolina Press), pp. 925–27.

Religion and Representation in the Filmic South

Gary W. McDonogh and Cindy Hing-Yuk Wong

As the credits roll, Robert Altman's 1975 film *Nashville* cuts from the opening white noise of a political van to two stereotypic icons of Altman's country music universe. The camera first closes in tightly on country music idol Haven Hamilton, recording his fervently Americanist ballad "We Must Be Doing Something Right to Last Two Hundred Years." Haven interrupts the studio's ambience to drive away the BBC journalist Opal, who acts throughout the movie as a satirical commentator for Altman. As the film cuts to Opal entering a second studio, a black gospel group from Fisk University commands the screen. The director, through Opal, focuses our attention on the anomaly of a white lead singer, who is Linnea Reese, wife of Hamilton's corrupt lawyer. Thus, in these introductory scenes, Altman has interwoven two mythic strands of southern identity: a nativist, revivalist patriotism and black evangelical religion; facile jingoism segues to "Do You Believe in Jesus?" on his complex soundtrack. Yet, at the same time, Altman has posed these with an ironic eye. Through its claustrophobic point of view, for example, the camera signals Hamilton's opportunism and intolerance. The black choir, by contrast, lacks any viewpoint: it is seen and heard rather than seeing. Opal's attempts to identify Reese with a missionary for patriotism, and to identify black Christians with an archetypical primitivism may irritate us or challenge our superiority as observer. Overall, however, Altman highlights how religion founders on the great southern divide of race, while framing it with questions of morality and authenticity.

Midway through the film, Altman returns to organized religion to arrange his many characters in a montage of four church scenes. A Catholic mass includes four characters: Lady Pearl, Hamilton's companion, who professes a fanatical devotion to the Kennedys and a disdain for the southern religious intolerance that rejected them; Sue-Lynn, an aspiring but untalented singer; her black companion; and a farmer deserted by his wife, Albuquerque. All have been drawn to Nashville by music dreams. Next, an unspecified white evangelical church hosts Haven Hamilton in in the barely integrated choir, and his lawyer who is stymied by the sign language with which his deaf children sing. A black church vignette returns to the original choir, an additional black country-western singer, and Linnea. Finally, the ever weak country heroine, Barbara Jean, becomes herself the focus of religious attention as she sings a solo at the front of a small hospital chapel. Seven other characters, all outsiders, are unaccounted for: Opal, for example, seeks symbolic meaning among school buses while two folk singers are shown in bed.

At the midpoint of his film, Altman has adopted a second meaning of southern religion to orient reading of his characters. Rather than expressing southern identity looking outward, defined by patriotism, race, religion, and accent, he has drawn upon organized religion as a system that classifies and divides. His South includes a range of religious beliefs that reflect internal divisions of race, class, and attitude while united in their orientation to vague American dreams.

As the film ends, the ever-renewed virgin, Barbara Jean, is shot—by camera and assassin—while on stage at a political fund-raiser at the Nashville Parthenon, the reproduction of the temple of the Virgin Athena in Athens, Greece. Haven is unmasked (unwigged) while screaming, "This isn't Dallas, it's Nashville." As others flee, Albuquerque, who had abandoned her husband in the first scene, hesitantly draws the crowd into the film's anthem of redemption which binds them into community: "(You May Say That I Ain't Free, But) It Don't Worry Me."

In contrast to his differentiation of organized religion at other key points, here Altman argues a message of death and redemption without any reference to specific church, creed, or liturgy. Yet the ending is as "religious" as any other part of the film in its sense of confrontation with transcendent issues and moral values, and Altman's choices or omissions here become just as meaningful. Indeed, critics have recognized death and transfiguration as a fundamentally religious attribute of Altman's films (Sarris and Haskell 1975).

For an ethnographic interpretation of this film in its relation to religion and the filmic South, we must raise four additional points. First,

Altman's complex text met with an equally complex reception. Reports from Nashville stressed the uncomfortable rejection of the film as the work of someone who did not understand the industry, the South, or the city: "Some of the younger musicians admired its hip humor (Willie Fong Young loved it), but the country music establishment's comments ranged from Webb Pierce's 'a nightmare' to Jeanne Pruett's 'It was hokey from start to finish' " (Anderson 1975:42). However, Neil O'Connell (1976), a Catholic chaplain at Fisk University, relished the experience of seeing the film in a suburban mall that only days previously had hosted a rally for Johnny Cash. He praised its authenticity in most details except for integration. Meanwhile, critics outside the South read *Nashville* as a parable about America in which the South itself became a signifier of deeper moral issues confronting society as a whole (Kael 1975; Pechter 1975; Gilliatt 1975; Marcus 1975; French 1981). Outside the United States, the film was taken as an intensely symbolic statement of America, without reference to the South as moral terrain (Behar 1975; Powell 1975).

Second, the text points to the formation of Altman himself as auteur. Born a Catholic in Missouri and educated by Jesuits, Altman jokingly admitted the possibility of religious influence decades after he stopped practicing any religion (Hitchens 1975; Macklin 1976; Wexman and Bisplinghoff 1984). O'Connell (1976:113) notes: "Altman tells us that the Nashville in 'Nashville' is a sacrament for the United States at the time of its Bicentennial. In this light, I and fellow Nashvillians would be too harsh to seek a literal presentation of Nashville in the film. But this is difficult for Nashvillians to avoid for they do live in the Vatican of the Bible Belt and religious fundamentalism. Southern Protestantism is devoid of the sacramentalism which Altman himself experienced in his younger years as a Catholic and which carries over into his films"[1] Many of Altman's films, from *That Cold Day in the Park* (1969) to *Vincent and Theo* (1990), concentrate on sacramental visions and questions of the meaning of truth, love, fall, and redemption.

Nashville, as its continuing references to the Kennedys insist, also sprang from a historical and filmic context. It represented a commentary on bicentennial hoopla as well as the aftermath of Vietnam. Yet, following Susan Jeffords's (1989) reading of the remasculinization of America in the transformation of tragedy into triumph in the post-Vietnam film,

Altman's film seems haunted by Vietnam without refighting it. Both civil religion and patriotic sacrifice nuance Altman's vision and commentary.

Finally, in filmic terms, *Nashville* also was phrased within a traditional genre—the "Southern"—on which it commented as well. Two other Altman films, *Thieves Like Us* (set in Depression-era Mississippi, 1974) and *Come Back to the Five and Dime, Jimmy Dean, Jimmy Dean* (1982) are easily classified therein. A fourth, the parable-fantasy *Brewster McCloud* (1970), set in Houston, is at least ambiguously southern.[2] Religious and moral references range from Brewster's Icarian (Adamic?) fall to the neon images of Jesus and Jimmy Dean that dominate the film of Altman's staging of the play. While Altman has performed similar excursions into Westerns, military life, and film noir, he has demonstrated an appreciation of the South as a moral universe. Religion and morality, we argue, are central to the Southern as genre.

Yet Altman's vision remains emblematic of the ambiguities that we have found in reviewing the meaning of religion as both church and transcendent moral quest in a range of feature films of the celluloid South. On the one hand, in *Nashville* Altman contrasts organized religion as a web of signifiers central to southern identity with a southern redemption whose spirituality ignores any creeds. On the other hand, he shares with many outside readers a sense that the South in all its cinematic motifs—plantation, natural primitivism, decadence—provides a moral stage through which questions of faith and morals might be appropriately represented for the nation as a whole. This bifocality becomes further intensified in the context of the social formation of the South as readership for such texts. What a southern viewer can classify as inaccurate, nasty, or silly within a universe in which church and morals have their spaces, not necessarily coincident, inverts the hegemonic perspective of those who read the South—and those who practice religion—in a literary, filmic, or even ethnographic fashion, as fictional others.

This essay cannot do justice to the range of films that address—and fail to address—religion, faith, and morals in the South or the many problems of definition of genre (see French 1981). Even were we to limit ourselves to modern films or to the classics that have been examined in primary texts such as *The Celluloid South*, *Media-Made Dixie*, or *Film and the South*, the range of feature films, their production, texts, readership, and impact remain vast. We have chosen, instead, to rely on data and analyses about religion in southern cultural and filmic identity. Our methods are best defined within a framework that originated in Great Britain under the rubric "cultural studies" in synthesis with ethnographic practice in the South and studies of American film. That is, we are concerned that our reading of films be meaningful within a framework that takes into account not only the seductions of the film as text but also the production, context, readership, and impact of films in the South and in the United States as a whole. This paper balances an overview of problems of religion in film and the genres of southern film which take on variable meanings with close readings of key films that we feel suggest the range and complexity of religion and film in the South. Our concentration on commercial films rather than documentaries reflects the composition of the symposium and volume as a whole. Nonetheless, similar contradictions are present in anthropologists' and documentarians' explorations of the South on and off film.

BACKGROUND AND METHODS

Our backgrounds as authors and anthropologists suggest differences in the formation of gaze that are intrinsic to our understanding of film. For Wong (1991), growing up in Hong Kong, southern films were simply "American" or even "Western." The readings created by localized American myths were, on the whole, absent. As her readings have become more nuanced with years of contact with the South, they have also been professionalized by the experience of anthropological film- and videomaking as well as by studies in film theory. For McDonogh, southern films entail at least a partial process of identification—*Birth of a Nation* was an uncle's favorite film, while he was dragged to see *Gone with the Wind* at Louisville's Rialto theater in the 1950s on its re-release. Since then, McDonogh (in press) has been engaged in active fieldwork on religion in Savannah, Ga., in which Wong has participated as critic.

Our different readings have heightened our awareness of many of the issues signalled by cultural studies and media analysts (Johnson 1987; Stuart 1989; Wallace 1990; Turner 1990). In particular, in this examination of southern films, we have asked not only about production and text but also about readership and incorporation of film imagery and myths into southern culture. Thus films raise questions we think of as being not merely filmic or literary but also central to anthropological analyses of the South. This model of reading, for example, can be contrasted with the limits imposed in a classic text on southern film, Jack Kirby's *Media-Made Dixie* (1978:xviii): "Finally, by *South* I mean mainly the white majority. Americans typically intend *southerner* as descriptive of whites only, unless they are distinguishing between blacks by region— then they are 'southern Negroes,' not southerners—and this book is about Americans' perceptions. But of course black southerners have played a vital role in the South and in whites' consciousness of role and region; so I have tried to account for the black South both in proportion and justice, too."

We suggest that both black and white readings constitute the South, along with those readings defined by other divisions of class, gender, and urbanism.[3] Even more, we are concerned to ask about the relationship between a pluralized "American" vision and a southern reading of films that may recognize, highlight, or criticize elements not generally treated in film criticism. A Jewish friend from New York, for example, told us that he hated *Driving Miss Daisy* because "those people seemed like Episcopalians." Wong found it a sentimentalized black-white relationship. To McDonogh and some other southerners it spoke to the position of dual minorities and critical voices within the liberal Jewish tradition of the South as well as to issues of gender and age often linked to family experience. All these readings form part of the construction of its "southernness."

Ultimately, this analysis becomes an approximation toward broader questions such as "What is South?" and "What are the roles of religion in southern life?" In general we will refer to southern films as those which use in a significant way the geographical settings of the Confederacy and border states, usually but not exclusively within subgenres established over decades in national filmmaking.[4] Religion, in our usage, includes both an organized community of the faithful responding to transcendence—a church—and an individualized or "secularized" wrestling with issues of morality, ethics, or transcendent truth. Moreover, we take this range of religious belief and practice to be fundamental to the social life and cultural definition of the South as a whole as well as to its divisions. At the same time we look to religious themes that may not be seen as typically southern, seeing the diversification of religion in the South as a social tapestry, a diversity of gifts, in James Peacock and Ruel Tyson's phrase (1989; see Reed 1981, 1983; McDonogh [in press]). Religion serves not only to unite, as the essentialist tradition of the South may put it, but also to divide and classify: black and white, Protestant and Catholic, Christian, Jew, Muslim, and Buddhist. This division also becomes a part of the representation and concealment of the filmic South, in both signifiers and audience. It is also necessary to ask about the relations of religion and film within which the South becomes a signifier.

Religion, for various reasons, has had an awkward filmic history. Despite the market for biblical films, or the depiction of ethnic bonds through church or synagogue, religion has been an uncomfortable theme for many American filmmakers. The desire to attract audiences while not offending anyone has made religion a sensitive issue. Thus the Motion Picture Production Code, for example, has a Jesuitical tone: "The motion pictures which are the most popular of modern arts for the masses, have their moral quality from the minds which produce them and from their effects on the moral lives and reactions of their audiences. This gives them a most important morality" (Mast 1982:322), or "In the use of this material, it must be distinguished between *sin* which by its very nature *repels* and *sin* which by its very nature *attracts*" (Mast 1982:325).[5]

Perhaps as a result of the pervasive influence of the code, religion recurs in veiled forms throughout movies, almost as an epiphenomenon of genre. Tales of ethnicity may have religious overtones, from *Abie's Irish Rose* (1946) to *Godfather III* (1990) or these may seem conspicuously absent, as in *Avalon* (1990). Religion does not necessarily coincide with transcendence, ethical dilemmas, or moral questions. In fact, an ethnic or religious movie can be as anodyne as any other popular film (May and Bird 1982; Miller 1978, 1980). Awareness of the peculiar relationship of religion and film provides still another overtone to any discussion of the "Southern" as a genre haunted by religion. Yet the questions we raise are not just problems of representation but also problems of ethnography and cultural analysis, in which film and social studies should be reunited. Both southern religion and the Southern as film, for example, share American cultural concerns with innocence, heterosexual binary love, "justice," individualism, and movement. These themes permeate both content and form, as critics such as Noel Burch (1990) and Jean Baudrillard (1988) have pointed out.

RELIGION, REPRESENTATION, AND GENRES IN THE SOUTHERN FILM

A first approximation to relations of religion and film can be made through discussion of major subgenres within the filmic South. In particular, we will look at plantation films, black films and black participation in mainstream films, and plain folk films ("hick flicks," see Austin 1981), following categories from Charles Wilson and William Ferris's *Encyclopedia of Southern Culture* (1989) as well as classic texts by Jack Kirby (1978), Edward Campbell (1981), and Warren French (1981). This leaves aside certain other identifiable genres, such as decadent/sexual repression films, police/chase films, musicals, war films, and "national problem" approaches. Even the rich category of preacher films is represented here only in passing, suggesting the need for future studies.

Plantation Scenes

One of the classic subgenres of southern films is the plantation film that evokes the moonlight and magnolias legend of the old South. As Edward Campbell notes, this was also one of the first refractions of the South to become established as a filmic myth: "As the early, predominantly urban motion picture theaters attracted ticket buyers eager for excitement, the romantic plantation image was perfect for a new medium; in very brief films the stories furnished escape with by-then instantly recognizable characters and settings" (1989:923). As represented by such films as *Birth of a Nation* (1915), *So Red the Rose* (1935), *Band of Angels* (1957), *Jezebel* (1938), and above all *Gone with the Wind* (1939), the plantation myth became as salient (and as cheap) on screen as in any other southern imagination (French 1981).

While the elements of the film—handsome cavaliers, petulant heroines, colorful slaves, and dramatic showpiece sets—are readily identifiable, so are the absences. Most of these films involve very little depiction of religion of any sort, just as they ignore much of city life and social diversity, nonslaveholders, and any means of production apart from agriculture. The absence of religion becomes apparent in a comparison of the cinematic treatment (David O. Selznick 1939) and novel of *Gone with the Wind* (Mitchell 1936). In her novel, Margaret Mitchell represented the marriage of the antebellum old South and the new South through the characters of the Irish Catholic immigrant Gerald O'Hara and the French Catholic Savannahian Ellen Robillard. Thus, Ellen Robillard epitomizes coastal old money and breeding, but she threatens her Presbyterian father that she will enter a convent unless he allows her to marry O'Hara (1936:36–37). At Tara, "the heartbreak and selflessness that she would have dedicated to the Church were devoted instead to the service of her child, her household and the man who had taken her out of Savannah and its memories and had never asked any questions" (1936:39). Through Scarlett's eyes, Ellen later takes on an identification with the Virgin Mary (1936:49), which adds another religious dimension to her martyr's death. On the whole, Scarlett's religion is rather more unclear—yet references recur in the novel, including Rhett's dismissal with "you haven't any religion left so the Church won't matter" (1936:711). Catholicism acts as both an ethical and ethnic marker (McDonogh [in press]).

In the film, the focus is narrowed, and the element of religious distinctiveness interwoven into the lengthy novel is reduced to brief visual references to a rosary and some other stereotypes of Irish ethnicity. The scene of the rosary is shifted from Ellen and the Virgin Mary to Scarlett's decision to pursue Rhett. Both the presence and causality of Catholicism and the meaning of religious diversity are reduced despite the presence of moral quests and ambiguities ranging from slavery to love and adultery. Indeed, one critic (Irvin 1983) has found as much earth mother goddess in the myth of *Gone with the Wind* as any other denomination (see also Pyron 1983; Taylor 1989). Does this reflect the demands of the film as genre, the reticence of filmmakers to deal with religion, or the conventions of representation of the plantation South as a whole?

Other films betray an even slighter presence of organized religion yet still retain a moral edge. In *Band of Angels* (1957), religion belongs to assembled slaves singing spirituals along the river, not to white spectators nor to the young girl whose life is ruined by the discovery of her mixed racial heritage, the moral center of the film. In *Jezebel* (1938), religious commentary is framed by peripheral characters and commentators on the heroine's actions. The film handles many of the same themes of love, evil, death, and redemption as *Gone with the Wind* but creates a New Orleans venue oddly devoid of Catholics (and scarcely noting creoles). Yet a liturgical quality permeates a crucial scene after the heroine, Julie, realizes that her former lover, Pres, has married. Having driven Pres away with her scandalous red ball gown, Julie knows that her unused white virginal dress will never become a wedding dress. Julie sits on the porch, surrounded by singing slaves, and comments to her Aunt Belle, "That's why I wore my white dress tonight; I'm being baptized."

Thereafter, religious symbolism becomes more potent. After the suicidal death of another of Julie's former beaus in a duel, her aunt names her "Jezebel" in reference to a destructive and brutally punished Israelite queen (1 Kings 17–21; 2 Kings 8–9). Finally, with ambiguous biblical reference (depending upon how one reads the meaning of Lazarus [Lazarette?] Island) Julie seeks redemption through the possibility of bringing life to her former lover or death to them both. Wong holds an alternate reading of Julie's triumph over the northern wife, recapturing the lover even at the price of her own life. Ida Jeter observed that the movie code precluded filming the original play's ending in which Pres admitted his love for Julie on the way to Lazarette; nevertheless, Jeter proposed a complex reading of personal and political redemption (1981).

Plantation films, like other southern genres, represent historical myths that entail selection and arrangement of elements for audiences of southerners and nonsoutherners. The omission of organized religion as a theme suggests an editing of both southern history and literary canons, even of basic works transmuted to the screen. The plantation provides a key scenario through which to enact the great moral question of the antebellum South—the meaning of slavery. Ironically, it is also a setting in which slavery and morality can be put aside to deal with romance and redemption in a "mythical" frame. These films point to the fundamental question of our analysis: not so much why formal religion is absent in *Gone with the Wind* or *Jezebel* as why death and redemption would be so clearly argued through use of a southern setting. They also raise questions about the relations of blacks and whites to the "Southern" as genre.

Black Films: The Other

As the introductory citation from Jack Kirby suggested, black films have not generally been read as a genre within southern films. Yet demographically, sociologically, and symbolically, the South was a black homeland in the United States well into the twentieth century. Hence, blacks are often incorporated as elements into southern films, whether plantation romances or indictments of racism. Moreover, the South has been a setting for black films, whether black in actors and text or actually black in control of production. From *Hallelujah* and *Green Pastures* in the 1930s to *The Color Purple* in the 1980s, the relationship between black life and the rural South has been central to black and white films and black and white audiences.

Blacks nevertheless often have been relegated to merely stereotypic roles in the Hollywood South. They portray repositories of faith, expressed publicly in dialogic interpolations, rituals, and, above all, music. Thus, in plantation films, blacks display a spirituality against which whites' actions can be judged. These values extended to all black films for white audiences, such as the first all black talkie, *Hallelujah*, although readership could be more complex than production.[6] White audiences tended to be patronizing and indulgent, as in a review (quoted in Noble 1948:53) in *Theatre and Film Illustrated*:

> From the very first shot of the cotton fields, where the coloured workers are heard singing at their work, the atmosphere of "Hallelujah" takes hold of one and one lives amongst and understands the people King Vidor is depicting. It can well be described as a song of the American Negro, in which are skillfully blended humour, pathos, sentiment, fervent religious emotions and equally fervent passion. The film is imbued with the revivalist spirit which, as it were, demonstrates the characters and films the main motif against which is played the drama of a Negro's love and emotions.

Religion here becomes a marker of both southernness and of black life as otherness. Thus, *Variety* warned provincial bookers that *Hallelujah* was part of the "popularization" of an urban tendency "to glorify the primitive negro life of the south and the emerging race consciousness and intellectual vigor of the colored people" (Cripps 1977:255ff).

Meanwhile, black critics responded with mixed feelings:

> Writers in the Negro Press considered, however, that "Hallelujah" was something of a step forward in the struggle for Negro expression on the screen and even such severe critics as W. E. B. DuBois admitted that it was beautifully staged under severe limitations and possessed commonsense and real life without the exaggerated farce and usual horse-play. But, as usual, opinion was divided and certain Negro film critics referred to "King Vidor's filthy hands reeking with prejudice," and to the film's "insulting niggerisms." Sections of the white press seemed to find the characterizations quite *amusing*. As the critic of the New York Times remarked: "The audience was especially amused by the baptism scene with a host of white-clad Hallelujah-rousing blacks standing on the side of the water ready to go through the baptism but evidently fearful of the ducking!" (Noble 1948:52).

As a moral conscience in all-black as well as plantation films, blacks became objects rather than subjects of film morality.

Race and gender also became intertwined. In plantation movies, for example, black women were the repositories of spirituals and spiritual wisdom, the moral interlocutors, but they could not change their own lives. As Hattie McDaniel found, this could convey an ambivalent stance in public as well as filmic life (Jackson 1990). Indeed, blacks became moral objects in a more striking way in a series of southern movies about civil rights, ranging from *To Kill a Mockingbird* (1962) to the recent but more objectifying *Mississippi Burning* (1988), which depicted blacks as passive, praying, and occasionally murdered moral objects over whom white antagonists from the North and South fought (see Wallace 1990:123–25). Yet, as preacher or mammy blacks in the South raised issues of conscience for the nation as spectators even without being allowed to assume their own spiritual or temporal action.

Interpretation of this tradition in the depiction of blacks becomes more complicated in *The Color Purple* (1985). In this case, a movie with a strong religious focus was condemned by many white critics and black male leaders. Andrea Stuart (1989) and Michele Wallace (1990), however, have suggested striking alternate readings from a feminist gaze. Stuart points to the importance of the self-realization of black women in the South and the possibility of a happy ending as a meaningful response to conditions of life. In terms of filmic translation of Alice Walker's womanist theology, Stuart (1989:73) criticizes a misinterpretation of the novel's spirituality:

> The politically subversive implications of love's redemptive power in Celie's self-realisation is translated into a pseudo-Christian individualism whereby the "worthy" individual gets her just reward. Spielberg takes this to the extreme in the reconciliation scene between the community's wayward woman (Shug) and its devout patriarch (her preacher father). This resembles nothing short of a cross between *The Wiz* and a revival meeting, and is easily the most irritating in the whole film, disillusioning those of us who thought, for once, we were to be spared another black musical.

On the whole, Stuart lauds the film for its representation of the black southern woman's experience, echoed in both its commercial success and the reception we have found for the film among blacks with whom we have discussed it at some length. The failure in the film's representation of the novelist's revolutionary viewpoint about God proves especially interesting in that women are marginalized from religion in much of the history of southern film although they may act as symbols of virginity, motherhood, or whoredom.

Wallace affirms Stuart's (1990:73) reading of the transformation of the novel: "In the movie, God the father is not deconstructed but reverified, contradicting the book in spirit as well as content." She also orients her reading towards stimuli for black thought—often in disagreement with the movie—that range from gender to cultural and racial iconicity. She also suggests readings of power and class that the film evades, again suggesting comparison with another facet of the "Southern" in which whites rather than blacks are oppressed.

Plain Folk of the Movies

Religion can also be used as a marker of southern traditional behavior, or even an indictment of primitiveness. Thus Stanley Kramer's *Inherit the Wind* (1962) begins with a female soloist singing "Give Me That Old-Time Religion" against a martial beat and minor overtones as community leaders cross the courtyard and enter the school. A song of southern evangelism is thus converted into an ominous threnody, setting the stage for the confrontation that immediately follows. The same song is then reorchestrated as a backdrop for collages of headlines through which the isolation of the community and regressiveness of its position is expressed ("What do we care what some foreigners and city slickers think?") and as a theme for a women's march through the streets of the city where evolution goes on trial. Meanwhile, E. K. Hornbeck, from Chicago, is an interlocutor who begins, with ironic references to religion, to set the tone of the viewer. For example, as he offers the heroine an apple, he explains, "Don't worry, I'm not the serpent little Eva; it's not from the tree of knowledge. You won't find one growing in Heavenly Hillsboro."

Other plainfolk films, which constitute a far-ranging category, include religion as a primary but often negative signifier from an outsider's gaze: the South as a problem for its backwardness, if not a nostalgic other defined by the values it clings to. Organized religion, even more than a moral or ethical sense, marks a separateness, a primitivism that substantiates other myths of rural plain folk. In Jean Renoir's *The Southerner* (1943), for example, the hero engages in a direct dialogue with God about all actions in his life amidst a complex French vision of the myth of the South (Wegner 1981; Bazin 1971). Less sympathetic portraits, in fact, occur in later movies about plain folk of the South, often entailing a direct involvement of the filmmaker. One thinks of John Sayles's portrayal of the fundamentalist West Virginia preacher who opposes the strike in *Matewan* (1987), or John Huston as the powerfully torturing patriarch of the early flashback in *Wise Blood* (1979).

The origins of this genre seem to receive less attention in filmographic studies than the flamboyance of the plantation South. Yet Noel Burch (1990:128) has pointed to the central tension between the potential disorder of an early plainfolk mayhem drama like *The Kentucky Feud* (1905) and the later "village" films and the works of D. W. Griffith in the formation of both narrative style and filmic representation in American cinema: "At Biograph it seems that when Griffith first joined them they had already developed a reassuring dramaturgy deriving from the homogenised melodrama still surviving at the beginning of the century and familiar to Griffith from this theatrical experience . . . Most of Griffith's Biograph films are explicitly addressed to two audiences: towndwellers who, although they may only have reached the city recently, still clung to a nostalgia for the 'lost paradise' of the village; and the rural audience itself, which was beginning to grow much more rapidly than was the case in France." The complex associations of religion, rurality, and backwardness continue in a remarkable number of contemporary films. *Winter People* (1983), a negligible retelling of Romeo and Juliet in the hills, proves as comfortable with the ambivalent motif of fundamentalism and bigotry as *Next of Kin* (1989), where religion is one more in an array of traditionalist values with which "hillbillies" confront the city. These films also include more secularized and popular films, from *Thunder Road* (1958) onward, in which plain folks become heroes against an unjust system (Real 1989:920–21).

Sergeant York (1941) provides a classic intertextual inversion of southern life and religion in the plainfolk film that confirms stereotypes by its rather sophisticated manipulation of them. The film begins with the dramatic confrontation between a simple preacher and gun-shooting rowdies outside: "appears to me the Devil be a-knockin' at the house of worship." A drunken Alvin York shoots his initials in the tree while his mother attends services, and the isolation of the valley is defined in the question of an outside salesman: "How do you fellows get into this valley?" Answer: "We're born here."

Conversion here forms a major dialogue between the preacher and Alvin York, expressed through folk preaching about "wrassling with Satan" and statements like "they ain't no use in a fellow goin' out lookin' for religion; it's just got to come to him," amidst scenes of hunting, plowing, and the general store. Finally, the lightning flash of a neo-Pauline conversion brings Alvin into his mother's church as "Give Me That Old-Time Religion" calls him to repentance before the congregation. Again, this hymn provides a recurring motif throughout the film.

Sergeant York is remarkable in its presentation as an apparent war film whose first half focuses on community and conversion in the Tennessee hills. Indeed, this premise is later turned against war in long dialogues of plain folk and sinfulness. Alvin's initial objection to war and killing provokes the first of these discussions within the community. In training camp, York and his officers pursue the theme by a scriptural debate simplifying many aspects of just-war theories. In the hills, these are reduced to off-stage echoes of "God" and "country" until he finds a way against a coda meshing hymns of Protestantism and civil patriotism. They reverberate through interpretation of York's heroism in France, where he killed (Germans) to keep more from dying (Americans). Then York returns humbly to his mother and his sweetheart in the hills.

Thus, to McDonogh and to some others with whom he talked about the film, *Sergeant York* became a startlingly pacifist film, an indictment of the United States in terms of southern religion. Yet this reading may reflect the weakening of any coherent pacifist position in contemporary films of a post-Vietnam ideology (see Jeffords 1989). Wong read it as a typical justification of American intervention rather than a religious dialogue: in the end, after all, York does kill and America wins the war. Different readings must be imputed to audiences of 1941. As Clayton Koppes (1987) has pointed out, *Sergeant York* appeared with government approbation and honor to veterans at a point when American entry into World War II was a theme of intense debate. Isolationists accused the film and the president, who invited York to the White House for a screening, of manipulation of the American people (Justus Doenecke, personal communication 1990; see also Koppes 1987; Lee 1981).

This agenda clarifies the meanings that southern religion and southern film had assumed. Even though generally a mark of primitivism, religion was still strongly associated with the South itself. Hence, the York biography provided an established scenario in which to argue a political point as much as a moral one (Lee 1981). Religion, like the South, becomes a straw man before the inevitability of intervention. This inversion brings us back to the genre as a whole and to the questions it raises for religion in the celluloid South: Who are these films made for? Who is the audience implied by the filmmaker and text? Several indications suggest that they are not self-referential or designed to appeal to a "plainfolk audience." One, already noted, is the involvement of the filmmaker in a striking but negative role. Another is the guidance of the interlocutor, who sets the stage with irony, sarcasm, and even philosophical arguments. The latter is played with in *Nashville*, when the interlocutor cannot be taken seriously. But how do the heroic tones of *Sergeant York* fit this framework? Multiple audiences, in fact, may find multiple texts and meanings through which to appropriate these genres. Here the analysis of individual films can provide an important counterpoint to a generic/cultural interpretation.

FILMS AS TEXTS: CLOSE READINGS

In order to look more deeply at film, religion, and representation, we end with three films that facilitate interesting perspectives on production, text, and readership. *Steel Magnolias* (1989) suggests questions about the emergence of religious themes in relation to another key area of interest for southern films, the nature of gender. An older film, *Cool Hand Luke* (1967), emphasizes the paradox of moral values and religious absence. Finally, *Nashville* as a "talking about religion" can be juxtaposed to the intensely religious and intensely southern *Wise Blood* (1979).

Women, Religion, and the South

In discussion of *The Color Purple*, we noted the reduction of women in southern films in contrast to religious beliefs and actions. Yet recent films such as *Driving Miss Daisy* (1989) and *Steel Magnolias* (1989) point specifically to the roles of southern women within religious scenarios. Both derive from plays by southern authors, which may contribute an important element to production as well as to reading. They have also been appropriated by the South as both stage representations and films.

Steel Magnolias, in particular, combines a profoundly liturgical framework that reiterates an archetypical "southern" theme of death and redemption with the diegesis of religion in everyday life while grappling with the ethical and moral issues of much of southern literature. That is, the film narrative is structured by interlocking cycles of liturgy and family history: Easter (marriage) to Christmas (pregnancy announcement) through Fourth of July (birth and rebirth through kidney transplant) and Halloween (marriage/death) to another Easter as a site of memories and rebirth. Each event is set slightly off screen, demanding that the viewer make a final association. These associations also prove complex: Halloween in the hometown marks a bridal shower and women's community while the isolated (married) daughter slides into a coma that will lead to her death. The film opens on the day before Easter, the Saturday of death, only to close a few years later on Easter itself, the resurrection.

The tension of liturgical organization, moral message, women's lives, and cinematic structure runs deep in the film. Crushed (Easter) eggs pose the problem of fertility at the beginning, while discovered (Easter) eggs frame the unexpected birth at the end. Early scenes move towards a center, the beauty parlor, in which women create their world faced with issues of love and death. Final scenes, outside and full of movement away from stage, open this world, completing the Easter resurrection.

Within this tightly ordered framework women talk, and even gossip, about communities and church in a notable range of religions that represent the variety of the South. While most characters assemble at the Presbyterian church for major events, the intruder beautician, Anelle, is absorbed into the group before undergoing a fundamentalist conversion experience that challenges her association with generally older (wiser) women. At the end, she moves back towards the center, following advice to "lighten up." Religion functions as a social signifier, characterized by asymmetrical portrayals of belief and practice. Not everyone believes, practices, or talks about God in the same way. Yet at the death of the young daughter, Shelby, her mother, M'lynn, asks of God the fundamentally religious question, "Why?" As in *The Color Purple*, the answer is found (insofar as there are answers) in the community of women and their choreography in crucial scenes.

Also striking in this film is the role of the wise woman as both source of knowledge and commentator, the interlocutory role often associated with the directorial male in other films. Here, the sense of wisdom and control is divided among all the senior women of the group, although their wisdom clearly dominates and comments on that of the hapless men in their lives.

A comparison to the black and southern womanism of *The Color Purple* would be interesting, especially since *Steel Magnolias* presents an adamantly white South in which blacks scarcely appear. Race and gender remain difficult themes to draw together. Even within "Southerns," *Driving Miss Daisy*, released in the same year as *Steel Magnolias*, links gender and race, but it deals with "extremes" beyond the orthodoxy of an offstage southern white evangelism. Miss Daisy is a Jew, whose religion and politics may be causes of suspicion to her socially conscious children. The synagogue in which she worships appears first as a source of her community with other Jews and later, at its bombing, as a symbol of community with her black chauffeur, Hoke, whose specific religious beliefs are curiously absent throughout the film. The other figure associated with religious practice is the housekeeper, whose death brings in the archetypical black gospel funeral. Also the rhetoric of Martin Luther King, Jr., is an indirect echo of blacks as both religious and morally conscious.

The intertextuality of the film also deserves more exploration, including the transmission of literary form in Robert Harling's play. We might evoke as well the contrastive secular female bonding of such "Northern" films as *The Women* (1939) or *Desperately Seeking Susan* (1985; Stacey 1989). These films also differ from the general insipid presence of women in the morally clearcut "Western." The wide acceptance of *Driving Miss Daisy* suggests the contrast between the religious overtones of an enclosed drama in the morally ambiguous South, which won a 1990 Oscar, with the 1991 award to the outdoor male/dyadic moral cleanliness of *Dances with Wolves*, which proved too Western for either of us.

Looking for an Absent Christ

Cool Hand Luke epitomizes a central paradox in the "Southern" with a conversion of Christology from an organized religious motif (although certain hymns linger in the background) to a strongly connotative portrait attributable to the South itself. Throughout the movie, Luke develops from an acerbic if aimless criminal, arrested for beheading parking meters, to a central figure in the prison community. His taunts and his escapes become vicarious resurrections for his friends/disciples—a photo of Luke in luxury on an escape becomes an icon for the camp. In the end, the identification of Luke with Christ is made explicit by the strong visual imagery of the cross imposed over the closing vision of the road gang. The torn picture of Luke himself (although a false icon for the men) is also superimposed. A critic develops this religious reading of a nonecclesial text, where parallels emerge slowly:

> An early shot, after he has fought the bully of the chain gang, shows him cowled with a white towel in a manner unmistakably resembling the conventional Bible picture. The other convicts become his disciples, and later betray him—he is punished for their misdeeds—his mother is brought to see him (in a van, for she is paralysed) and reproaches him for having left her. The extraordinary egg-eating sequence concerns the symbolic source of life, and an act of eating performed as more than the mere consumption of food. At the end of the film Luke, escaping the camp, finds refuge in a deserted chapel, his Gethsemane, and talks to God. In the course of Luke's capture and death, the mirrored spectacles of the sinister overseer are broken, symbolically foretelling the end of his reign of blind brutality. The purpose and ethics are alike obscure (Butler 1969: 156–57).

Another critic, who considers the film a type for the Christ allegory, adds: "The mythic fiction mode is apparent in the closing scene of the film as the prisoners gather in the recreation yard and with nostalgic fondness recall—the imaginative embroidering, of course—the feats Luke performed and how he, the captive, was always ahead of his captors. A kind of resurrection is implied in this scene. As the Christ of Faith lives on in his followers and, for many Christians, in a glorified state, so Luke has a timeless place in the hearts and minds of those who know him and would keep his memory alive" (Hurley 1982:71). Hurley's "kind of resurrection," like the movie's insistent closing crucifixion imagery and Butler's intensive interpretation, also points to the intricacies of religious film. Scattered yet insistent denotata have oriented critics toward Christocentrism, as if a modern Jesus would naturally be found in a Florida work camp. But is the moral content Christ-centered, an inversion of Christian messages? What does allegory gain if, writes Ivan Butler (1969: 157), "the purpose and ethics are alike obscure?"

The absence of Christ and Christianity is not unique to this film. Harper Lee's *To Kill a Mockingbird* became a powerful discussion of right and wrong that endures to this day. Yet, once again, the role of religion has diminished from book to film. An atmosphere permeated by civil religion is thus converted to one in which moral issues are argued in a rational voice. In this process the black preacher changes from a religious voice to the only religious representation and, at times, merely a religious object.

Both *Cool Hand Luke* and *To Kill a Mockingbird* use the South as the intrinsic locus for moral argument. In the latter, as a film transformation of a southern book, elements of organized religion are generally stripped away from white characters although retained as signifiers in the depiction of blacks. "It's a sin to kill a mockingbird" expresses a morality since "they don't do one thing but sing their heart out for us." But what is the message of this film if reduced to the simple maxim of "don't hurt those who hurt no one"? In the second, religion provides a framework instead of a central argument. Again, the ethical question seems obscure, perhaps as befitting a southern film.

Religion and the Heart of the South

Our paper opened with Robert Altman's *Nashville*, in which various facets of a religious imagination are woven into the multiple voices and narratives of the film, within a shimmering range of religious and moral questions that Altman has asked of the South through his career. To close, we will contrast that film with another recognized for both the profound religiosity of its novelistic source and the power of its filmic image: Flannery O'Connor's *Wise Blood*.

Wise Blood, in fact, proved a powerful if independent vision of O'Connor's novel, adapted with an extraordinary fidelity to the novel itself. We follow Hazel Motes from his escape from family and army to the city and the spiralling intricacies of his search for a sacramental truth. Motes, in the film, appears from the beginning to be marked by clothes and kinesics. Yet his outbursts become powerfully envisioned as he proclaims the Church Without Christ Crucified in a desperate and destructive alternative to the South.

As in other films of the South, sensuality, sin, and religion become one, if at times, offstage. For example, in Carson McCullers's original text of *Reflections in a Golden Eye* (book 1941; movie 1967), the sexual problems of a young soldier, which provide a catalyst for the stew of repressions and expressions on the army base, are attributed to the influence, once again, of fundamentalism. Although the film retains these sexual themes (in a lurid and suggestive way that circumvented the movie code), the specific reference to religion as a cause of problems is dropped, presumably acceding to code standards. In fact, the young soldier's actions are left without any motivation, intensifying the surrealism of the film.

The relationship of religion, pain, and sexuality in other films, such as *Wise Blood*, generally points to a judgment about religion (fundamentalism) from an implicit stance of an outsider and perhaps an appeal to the same judgment on the part of audiences. Yet the film's religious vision is also constructed within a myth of the South as a concrete, almost primal, locus of sexuality, sensual profusion, and expression as exemplified in this interaction of Motes with a supposedly blind street preacher and his daughter:

MOTES: I followed her because I wanted to say I wasn't beholden on her fast eye like she give me back there.
DAUGHTER: What do you mean? I never looked at you with no fast eye.
HAWKES: Shut up! No one could follow you. I can hear the urge of Jesus in his voice.
MOTES (sneering): Jesus! (spits)
HAWKES: Now you listen to me, boy. Jesus is a fact. You can't run away from Jesus.

MOTES: Now you listen to me. I come a long way since I believe in anything. I came halfway around the world.
HAWKES: You ain't come so far that you can keep from followin' me. Some preacher's left his mark on you. Did you follow me to take it off or for me to put on another one?

Both Flannery O'Connor's strong text (1949) and a filmic myth of the South have left a preacher's mark on the movie as well. If *Nashville* and Altman proved too rich a point with which to begin, *Wise Blood* seems an equally difficult if necessary point at which to end. One cannot escape, through either visualization or printed text, O'Connor's vision of the South as Christ-haunted, more than Christ-centered. Yet in this most religious of southern films, religion is insistently deconstructed as a meaningful system; even a Hazel shreds his flesh and burns out his eyes in the search for transcendence.

Hazel Motes's life thus becomes a prismatic reflection of Barbara Jean's death in *Nashville*. In one, a southern Christ lives a tortured life; in the other, a southern Virgin dies a tortured death. In both, we see the South as an intrinsic element—neither scenario nor symbol but element—in the development of the religious argument of the texts.

In his overview of film images of the South in the *Encyclopedia of Southern Culture*, Maurice Yacowar has perceptively noted that "Hollywood has presented the South as a corrupted Eden, dwelling first on an idyllic image and later on harsher ('realistic') vision. Throughout, the treatment of the South centers upon the tension between a mythic ideal and a severely flawed reality" (1989:925).[7] These observations on the *representation* of the South present interesting echoes of C. Vann Woodward's (1960:20–21) explorations of the soul of the region: "Much of the South's intellectual energy went into a desperate effort to convince the world that its peculiar evil was actually a 'positive good,' but it failed even to convince itself. It writhed in the torment of its own conscience until it plunged into a catastrophe to escape. The South's preoccupation was with guilt, not with innocence, with the reality of evil, not with the dream of perfection. Its experience in this respect, as in several others, was on the whole a thoroughly un-American one." Both these citations situate a broad religious consciousness at the heart of the southern experience. Yet, while the second voice is a southerner trying to understand his own heritage (if from a northern vantage), the first refers to filmic representation *of* the South by others for others. Between reality and representation, we return to the image of southern religion in film.

The representation of religion within "Southerns" accommodates to this moral preserve as well as the tortured history of Hollywood depiction of any religious element. What do these films, then, ultimately tell us about the South, or about the relationship of the South and film? However rich as ethnographic sources, they are hardly documents from southern culture nor even American ethnographic documents about a culture. We have argued as a major point that the South is portrayed as being an intrinsically "religious" domain even though its own representations of religion may be absent or demeaned in major film genres or distorted in conjunction with other cultural categories of race, gender, and class. We suggest further exploration around several central points.

First, films situate and in fact define the South within the moral and religious geography of American culture. This creation of the South has been a long-term process where the intersection of local culture and national domination has been played out in a historical succession of mass media. Here Paul Gaston's *The New South Creed* (1970) or Thomas Connelly's *The Marble Man* (1977) provide important possibilities for future comparison. Ethnographic study of film as ideology entails issues of production and text, which we have phrased within a cultural studies model. Issues of the ethnography of production as pioneered by Hortense Powdermaker (1951) might well be added, especially given the commitment of major studios to Florida for production. Or an anthropological gaze might be recast on D. W. Griffith as Kentuckian and producer (French 1981).

Second, films point to the differentiation of the South from American culture. The issue of readership, the ways in which films create their audience and indeed seem to limit their audience to the South, parts of the South, or the non-South, seems to us to be a particularly rich key to ethnographic readings. As cultural studies analysts have suggested, these readings must also be linked to appropriation of lived culture. *Birth of a Nation* and *Gone with the Wind* are artifacts and facets of southern culture as well as texts (Pyron 1983; Taylor 1989).

Third, films raise questions of what constitutes the South between the abstract myth and the concrete viewer. Consider the situation of blacks: can they be excluded as spectators, as actors in the lived culture of the South? Kirby's heuristic limitation of the South is not apparent in filmic representations and, we would suggest, challenges our construction of a united or differentiated southern culture. Gender raises some similar questions. Women have an ambivalent role in many of the films we have watched as natural guardians of life and death (M'Lynn in *Steel Magnolias*), stimuli to ethical dilemmas (Jezebel), or refuges of good (Mother York). Yet their power to reason, to understand, to be *theological,* is consistently underrated. Is this a cultural myth of everyday life, of the domestic being in opposition to the spectacles of male bonding (Jeffords 1989). The situation of women and religion in southern film recalls the paradoxes of the South itself.

Finally, this paper suggests a methodological need for complex reading and rereading of mass culture by anthropologists of the South. Scene by scene, text against text, representation against experience, this remains a rich area for future work. We can only admire the pioneers— especially without the VCR—and look forward to more discussion.

During the 1991 Academy Awards, former President Ronald Reagan explained his enthusiasm for "Westerns" on the basis of their clearcut morality: "The good guys win. The bad guys lose." How could we capture this elegance with regard to the "Southern" as a moral genre? We would suggest that our formulation would be more complex: "The good guys, if there are any, are tortured by guilt and sin and either become destroyed or find some painful but wisening redemption; the bad guys undergo much the same process, but also win from time to time." The filmic South amidst a plurality of readings has become a locus of moral ambiguity for the cinema of a nation, while many of its own questions of religion are only recently being explored. Religion and representation thus pose exciting problems for cultural and ethnographic analysts of the South.

NOTES

This paper has profited from comments at the Southern Anthropological Society meetings, including those of Karl Heider, Jon Anderson, and other participants. We have also gained insight from discussions with participants in the New College Cultural Studies Group, including Catherine Molteno, Mike Serulneck, Christian Perez, Marla Perez, and Steve Witt, and from conversations with Tom Wilson, Justus Doenecke, and Eugene Lewis. It would also have proved impossible without the assistance and commentary of Bill Woolridge at Renaissance Video.

1. O'Connell (1976:113) also observes the sullenness with which the local audience greeted Lady Pearl's open attacks on anti-Catholicism in the Kennedy era. Catholic sociologist Andrew Greeley (1976:2, 4) disagreed with his assessment, however, launching a diatribe against all American filmmakers for their lack of spirituality vis-à-vis Europeans: "Thus the belly dance in front of the Madonna's statue in 'Nashville' does not have the same symbolic impact as the giant crucifix being flown over the sundeck in 'La Dolce Vita.' The former juxtaposes the sacred and the sexual for our trivial amusement; the latter challenges us to wonder about the depths of the ambiguities of human life."

2. Points one might adduce apart from location include the early insistence on a patriotic and racist Daphne trying to sing "The Star-Spangled Banner" while being drowned out by "Lift Ev'ry Voice and Sing." The equally southern figure of Abraham Wright (supposed brother of the inventors of the airplane in Kitty Hawk, North Carolina) shows class and racial attitudes that also fit southern stereotypes. Perhaps the Sunbelt is, after all, harder to define and delimit, however southern (see Miller and Pozzetta 1988). Altman's *Health*, set in a convention in St. Petersburg, may also be a Sunbelt film, but we were unable to review it.

Altman's use of southern genres should be situated as well within his appeal to readily iconic American genres throughout his "American" films—the war film (*Mash*), the gangster film/film noire (*The Long Good-Bye*), and the "Western" (*McCabe and Mrs. Miller*, *Buffalo Bill and the Indians*), each with his unique twist. This leaves apart his so-called European films, most recently, *Vincent and Theo*.

3. The black historian Nell Painter (1991:49) has made a similar critique of the view of W. J. Cash's *Mind of the South* (1941): "Cash wrote of 'the mind' of the South without envisioning that women and black people might have a capacity to reason independently. . . . Like so much writing from the American intellectual tradition before civil rights and black studies movements, *The Mind of the South* was not intended for eyes like mine. Writing to fellow white North Carolinians, educated white Southerners, and northern book buyers, Cash never conceived of any but the most informal black or female critics."

4. Texas has had a unique position as the site of both "Southerns" and "Westerns." A similar ambiguity, however, seems to appear in a Florida that can host both *Body Heat* (1986) and *Edward Scissorhands* (1990).

5. The code becomes even more explicit in reference to organized religion:

(1) No film or episode in a film should be allowed to *throw ridicule* on any religious faith honestly maintained.

(2) *Ministers of religion* in their characters of ministers should not be used in comedy, as villains, or as unpleasant persons. [*Note:* The reason

for this is not that there are not such ministers of religion but because the attitude toward them tends to be an attitude toward religion in general.]

Religion is lowered in the minds of the audience because it lowers their respect for the ministers. *Ceremonies* of any definite religion should be supervised by someone thereby conversant with that religion (Mast 1982:331).

6. For example, studio publicity for the plantation film *So Red the Rose* (1935) adopted a remarkably patronizing tone, noting that Vidor found blacks difficult to work with since they were "fundamentally living only for the joy they get out of life" (Noble 1948:65).

7. Yacowar adds a point that we, too, have found interesting: "Perhaps because the industry knew it was dealing with a national myth, the most important film representations of the South have been adaptations of literary works" (1989:925). This seems to provide an interesting verisimilitude based in production to *Inherit the Wind*, *To Kill a Mockingbird*, *Wise Blood*, *Driving Miss Daisy*, and *Steel Magnolias*. But it does not explain the power of Altman's films nor the notable failures of the adaptation of some major authors to film, especially in the works of William Faulkner.

REFERENCES

ANDERSON, PATRICK, 1975. The Real Nashville. *New York Times Magazine*, August 31, New York edition, Sec. 6, pp. 10, 40–43.

AUSTIN, WADE, 1981. The Real Beverly Hillbillies. In French, ed., *The South and Film*, pp. 83–94.

BAUDRILLARD, JEAN, 1988. *America* (London: Verso).

BAZIN, ANDRE, 1971. *Jean Renoir* (New York: Simon and Schuster).

BEHAR, HENRI, 1975. Nashville. *Image et son*, no. 301 (December): 97–99.

BENAYOUN, ROBERT, 1975. Altman, U.S.A. *Postif*, no. 176 (December): 30–37.

BIRD, MICHAEL, 1982. Film as Hierophany. In May and Bird, eds., *Religion in Film*, pp. 3–22.

BLAKE, RICHARD A., 1975. Movies and Myths of America. *America* 133: 71–73.

BURCH, NOEL, 1990. *Life to Those Shadows* (Berkeley: University of California Press).

BUTLER, IVAN, 1969. *Religion in the Cinema*. International Film Guide Series (New York: A. S. Barnes).

CAMPBELL, EDWARD D. C., 1981. *The Celluloid South: Hollywood and the Southern Myth* (Knoxville: University of Tennessee Press).

———, 1989. Film and Plantation. In Ferris and Wilson, eds., *Encyclopedia of Southern Culture*, pp. 922–23.
CARDULLO, ROBERT J., 1976. The Space in the Distance: Robert Altman's Nashville. *Literature/Film Quarterly* 4:313–25.
CASH, WILBUR, J., 1941. *The Mind of the South* (New York: Knopf).
CONNELLY, THOMAS, 1977. *The Marble Man: Robert E. Lee and His Image in American Society* (New York: Knopf).
CRIPPS, THOMAS, 1977. *Slow Fade to Black: The Negro in American Film, 1900–1942* (New York: Oxford University Press).
———, 1978. *Black Films as Genre* (Bloomington: Indiana University Press).
DEMOTT, BENJAMIN, 1975. Superflick. *Atlantic* 236 (4):101–2.
FRENCH, WARREN, ed., 1981. *The South and Film* (Jackson: University of Mississippi Press).
GASTON, PAUL, 1970. *The New South Creed* (New York: Knopf).
GILLIATT, PENELOPE, 1975. Love and Death and Nashville. *The New Yorker*, June 16, pp. 107–9.
GREELEY, ANDREW, 1976. Hollywood and the God Question. *New York Times*, January 18, New York edition, Sec. 2, p. 1.
HITCHENS, GORDON, 1975. Kael on Catholic Directors, Jewish Comics, U.S. Enmity to Women, Minelli, Streisand. *Variety* 279 (5):26.
HURLEY, NEIL P., 1982. Cinematic Transformations of Jesus. In May and Bird, eds., *Religion and Film*, pp. 61–78.
IRVIN, HELEN, 1983. Gea in Georgia: A Mythic Dimension in *Gone with the Wind*. In Pyron, ed., *Recasting: Gone with the Wind in American Culture*, pp. 57–68.
JACKSON, CARLTON, 1990. *Hattie: The Life of Hattie McDaniel* (Lanham, Mo.: Madison Books).
JEFFORDS, SUSAN, 1989. *The Remasculinization of America: Gender and the Vietnam War* (Bloomington: Indiana University Press).
JETER, IDA, 1981. *Jezebel* and the Emergence of the Hollywood Tradition of a Decadent South. In French, ed., *The South and Film*, pp. 31–46.
JOHNSON, ROBERT, 1987. What Is Cultural Studies Anyway? *Social Text* 3:38–80.
KAEL, PAULINE, 1975. Coming: Nashville. *The New Yorker*, March 3, 1975, pp. 79–93.
KIRBY, JACK TEMPLE, 1978. *Media-Made Dixie: The South in the American Imagination* (Baton Rouge: Louisiana State University).
KOPPES, CLAYTON, 1987. *Hollywood Goes to War* (New York: Free Press).
LEE, DAVID, 1981. Appalachia on Film: The Making of *Sergeant York*. In French, ed., *The South and Film*, pp. 207–21.
LEE, HARPER, 1960. *To Kill a Mockingbird* (Philadelphia: J. B. Lippincott).

MCCULLERS, CARSON, 1941. *Reflections in a Golden Eye* (Cambridge: Riverside Press).

MCDONOGH, GARY, in press. *Black and Catholic in Savannah* (Knoxville: University of Tennessee Press).

MACKLIN, F. ANTHONY, 1976. The Artist and the Multitudes are Natural Enemies. *Film Heritage* 12:1–23.

MARCUS, GREIL, 1975. Ragtime and Nashville: Failure-of-America Fads. *Village Voice* 20 (31):61–62.

MAST, GERALD, ed., 1982. *The Movies in Our Midst: Documents in the History of Film in America* (Chicago: University of Chicago Press).

MAY, JOHN R., and MICHAEL BIRD, eds., 1982. *Religion in Film* (Knoxville: University of Tennessee Press).

MAY, JOHN R., 1982. Visual Story and the Religious Interpretation of Films. In May and Bird, eds., *Religion in Film*, pp. 23–43.

MILLER, RANDALL M., ed., 1978. *Ethnic Images in American Film and Television* (Philadelphia: The Balch Institute).

———, 1980. *The Kaleidoscope Lens: How Hollywood Views Ethnic Groups* (Englewood, N.J.: Jerome S. Ozer).

MILLER, RANDALL, and GEORGE POZZETTA, eds., 1988. *Shades of the Sunbelt* (Westport, Conn.: Greenwood).

MITCHELL, MARGARET, 1936. *Gone with the Wind* (New York: Macmillan).

NOBLE, PETER, [1948] 1969. *The Negro in Films* (Port Washington, N.Y.: Kennikat Press).

O'CONNELL, NEIL J., 1976. On Seeing *Nashville* in Nashville. *Commonweal* 103:115–18.

O'CONNOR, FLANNERY, 1949. *Wise Blood* (New York: Farrar, Straus & Giroux).

PAINTER, NELL, 1991. A Special Alien Group. In *Of Different Minds*, Eric Bates, ed. *Southern Exposure* 29 (Spring): 49–50.

PARRILL, WILLIAM, 1982. Robert Altman. In May and Bird, eds., *Religion in Film*, pp. 135–41.

PEACOCK, JAMES, and RUEL W. TYSON, JR., 1989. *Pilgrims of Paradox* (Washington: Smithsonian Institution Press).

PECHTER, WILLIAM, 1975. Trashville. *Commentary* 60:72–75.

PETERSON, RICHARD A., 1976. Nashville and America in One Dimension. *Society* 13 (January–February):90–95.

POWDERMAKER, HORTENSE, 1951. *Hollywood: The Dream Factory* (Boston: Little, Brown).

POWELL, DILYS, 1975. Altman's Triumph. *The Times* (London), September 21, p. 36.

Pyron, Darden Asbury, 1983. *Recasting: Gone with the Wind in American Culture* (Miami: University Presses of Florida).

Real, Jere, 1989. Film, "Hick Flick." In Wilson and Ferris, eds., *Encyclopedia of Southern Culture*, pp. 920–21.

Reed, John Shelton, 1981. The Same Old Stand. In *Why the South Will Survive*, by Fifteen Southerners (Athens: University of Georgia Press), pp. 13–34.

———, 1983. *Southerners: The Social Psychology of Sectionalism* (Chapel Hill: University of North Carolina Press).

Rockwell, John, 1975. It's Country Music, But the Best It Isn't. *New York Times*, June 13, New York edition, Sec. 2, p. 24.

Sarris, Andrew, and Molly Haskell, 1975. A Critic's Duet on *Nashville*. *Village Voice* 20 (23):81–82.

Stacey, Jackie, 1989. Desperately Seeking Difference. In Lorraine Gamman and Margaret Marshment, eds., *The Female Gaze: Women as Viewers of Popular Culture* (Seattle: Real Comet Press), pp. 112–29.

Stuart, Andrea, 1989. *The Color Purple:* In Defence of Happy Endings. In Gamman and Marshment, eds., *The Female Gaze: Women as Viewers of Popular Culture*, pp. 60–75.

Taylor, Helen, 1989. *Scarlett's Women: Gone with the Wind and Its Female Fans* (New Brunswick: Rutgers University Press).

Turner, Graeme, 1990. *British Cultural Studies: An Introduction* (Boston: Unwin Hyman).

Tyson, Ruel W., James Peacock, and Daniel W. Patterson, eds., 1988. *Diversities of Gifts: Field Studies in Southern Religion* (Urbana: University of Illinois Press).

Wallace, Michele, 1990. *Invisibility Blues: From Pop to Theory* (London: Verso).

Wegner, Hart, 1981. A Chronicle of Soil, Seasons and Weather: Jean Renoir's *The Southerner*. In French, ed., *The South and Film*, pp. 58–69.

Wexman, Virginia Wright, and Gretchen Bisplinghoff, 1984. *Robert Altman: A Guide to Reference and Resources* (Boston: G. K. Hall).

Wilson, Charles Reagan, and William Ferris, eds., 1989. *Encyclopedia of Southern Culture* (Chapel Hill: University of North Carolina Press).

Wong, Cindy H., 1991. Ritual Revisited. In R. Leong, ed., *Moving the Image: Independent Asian Pacific-American Media Arts* (Los Angeles: Visual Communications), pp. 204–5.

Woodward, C. Vann, 1960. *The Burden of Southern History* (Baton Rouge: Louisiana State University Press).

Yacowar, Maurice, 1989. Film Images. In Wilson and Ferris, eds., *Encyclopedia of Southern Culture*, pp. 925–27.

FILMOGRAPHY

Abie's Irish Rose (1946). 96 min. United Artists. Dir. Edward Sutherland.
Avalon (1990). 126 min. Tri-Star Pictures. Dir. Barry Levison.
Band of Angels (1957). 127 min. Warner Bros. Dir. Raoul Walsh. Based on a novel by Robert Penn Warren.
Bells of St. Mary's (1946). 126 min. RKO. Dir. Leo McCarey.
Birth of a Nation (1915). 185 min. Epoch. Dir. D. W. Griffith.
Body Heat (1981). 113 min. Warner. Dir. Fred Gallo.
Brewster McCloud (1970). 105 min. MGM. Dir. Robert Altman. Screenplay by D. W. Cannon.
The Color Purple (1985). 152 min. Warner/Amblin. Dir. Steven Spielberg. Novel by Alice Walker.
Come Back to the Five and Dime, Jimmy Dean, Jimmy Dean (1982). 110 min. Viacom. Dir. Robert Altman. From a play and screenplay by Ed Graczyck. Based on a play directed by Robert Altman.
Cool Hand Luke (1967). 126 min. Warner Bros. Dir. Stuart Rosenberg.
Dances with Wolves (1990). 181 min. Orion. Dir. Kevin Costner.
Desperately Seeking Susan (1985). 104 min. Orion. Dir. Susan Seidelman.
Driving Miss Daisy (1989). 99 min. Warner Bros. Dir. Bruce Bereford.
Edward Scissorhands (1990). 100 min. 20th Century Fox. Dir. Tim Burton.
Godfather III (1990). 163 min. Paramount. Dir. Francis Ford Coppola.
Gone with the Wind (1939). 220 min. MGM. Dir. Victor Fleming. Novel by Margaret Mitchell.
The Green Pastures (1936). 93 min. Warner. Dir. William Keighley.
Hallelujah (1929). 106 min. MGM. Dir. King Vidor.
I Am a Fugitive from a Chain Gang (1932). 90 min. Warner. Dir. Mervin LeRoy.
Inherit the Wind (1960). 127 min. United Artists. Dir. Stanley Kramer, with a screenplay by Nathan Douglas and Harold Jacob Smith. Based on a play by Jerome Lawrence and Robert Lee.
In the Heat of the Night (1967). 109 min. United Artists. Dir. Norman Jewison.
Jezebel (1938). 104 min. Warner. Dir. William Wyler.
The Kentucky Feud (1905). 675 feet. American Mutuoscope & Biograph Company. Ph. G. W. Bitzer.
Marjoe (1972). 88 min. Cinema V. Dir. Howard Smith and Sarah Kernochen.
Matewan (1987). 130 min. Cinecom International. Dir. John Sayles.
Mississippi Burning (1988). 120 min. Orion. Dir. Alan Parker.
Nashville (1975). 159 min. Paramount. Prod. and Dir. Robert Altman. From a screenplay by Joan Tewsbury.
Next of Kin (1989). 111 min. Warner Bros. Dir. John Irvin.
Night of the Hunter (1955). 93 min. United Artists. Dir. Paul Gregory.

Ode to Billy Joe (1976). 106 min. Warner. Dir. Max Baer.
Reflections in a Golden Eye (1967). 108 min. Warner Seven Arts. Dir. John Huston.
Sergeant York (1941). 134 min. Warner. Dir. Howard Hawkes.
The Southerner (1945). 91 min. United Artists. Dir. Jean Renoir.
Steel Magnolias (1989). 118 min. Tri-Star Pictures. Dir. Herbert Ross. Based on a screenplay and play by Robert Haring.
Suddenly Last Summer (1959). 114 min. Columbia. Dir. Joseph Mankiewicz.
Sugarland Express (1974). 110 min. Universal. Dir. Steven Spielberg.
Thieves Like Us (1974). 123 min. Universal. Dir. Robert Altman.
Thunder Road (1958). 92 min. United Artists. Dir. Arthur Ripley.
To Kill a Mockingbird (1962). 129 min. Universal-International. Dir. Robert Milligan.
Winter People (1988). 110 min. Orion. Dir. Ted Kotcheff.
Wise Blood (1979). 108 min. New Line. Dir. John Huston.
The Women (1939). 132 min. MGM. Dir. George Cukor.

Scenes from a Dream: (Nearly) Lost Images of Black Entertainers

Alex Albright

Lord-Warner Picture's 1948 black cast musical comedy featurette *Pitch a Boogie Woogie* was never intended as documentary. It was to be the cornerstone of John Warner's dream to build a Hollywood-East in Greenville, North Carolina. It was supposed to make him enough money on which to build a film empire. Its box office and artistic failures would probably have made it little more than a cinematic footnote had it not been for several factors Warner could never have recognized at the time. Representing so many variant images of the South that collided in the summer of 1947, *Pitch* is an intriguing cultural artifact. Rendered in a near-documentary style, the film depicts the sometimes startling and coincidental convergence of several aspects of African-American culture captured in Warner's crude and naive cinematic fashion. *Pitch* is a black-and-white look at an era that the South divided into black and white in the biggest of ways. Questions of race abound in every facet of *Pitch*: segregated towns and movie theaters; race films and the depiction of blacks in American cinema; the end of black vaudeville and minstrelsy; the shift from big band–style jazz to small combo bebop; and the relationships between white promoters and black entertainers.

Postwar Greenville, like most of the South, was still very much two separate towns, black and white, separated by the railroad tracks. But the black section, anchored by "the Block," was "a young New York town," Mattie Sloan recalls (Albright 1988). Blacks from all over eastern North Carolina were drawn there to work in the thriving tobacco industry and to enjoy the entertainments offered in Warner's Plaza The-

Publicity poster of *Pitch a Boogie Woogie*. Greenville, North Carolina, residents and costars Tom Foreman (*left*) and Herman Forbes. (Courtesy of Herman Forbes)

ater and in the numerous warehouse dances that featured all the biggest names in black entertainment.[1]

Because Greenville's segregated black community was still thriving in the 1940s and because Warner still packed his theater every time he showed a black cast film, he was unaware of national trends that were moving away from race films and racially separate theaters. White theater owners elsewhere had begun to recognize the business advantages of bringing blacks into their theaters. Black performers, particularly such marquee names as Lena Horne, Hazel Scott, Louise Beavers, Ethel Waters, and Dorothy Dandridge, were being cast in higher budget Hollywood films. By the time *Pitch* was released, in January 1948, the race film industry was virtually dead, and most of the black audience theaters that had made it possible were closed or failing.

As a film, *Pitch* is clearly inferior to such similarly formatted Hollywood box office successes as *Stormy Weather*. It is a simple 1930s-style backstage musical—a couple of characters dream of opening a night-

Evelyn Whorton, emcee of the dream nightclub in *Pitch*, was a featured star of Irvin C. Miller's "Brownskin Models." (Still taken from the original 35mm nitrate by Patrick Keough)

club, and their dream, filled with song and dance, becomes the movie. But *Pitch* also presents much harsher images than those one sees on the stage. It is about the Jim Crow South that, to a large part, made the race film industry possible and allowed shows such as Emerson S. Winstead's "Winstead's Mighty Minstrels" and Irvin C. Miller's "Brownskin Models," both featured in *Pitch*, to still earn a living on the road in the rural South, where they'd been relegated to play since the early 1930s. These were troupers who, even after race films were no longer in production, kept alive the entertainment forms they had perfected in the early 1920s. Several of the tent shows hung on into the mid-1950s. "Rabbit's Foot Minstrels," "Silas Green from New Orleans," and "Winstead's Mighty Minstrels" lasted several years after black vaudeville shows like Miller's had died, before they themselves were finally absorbed into larger white-owned carnivals as sideshows.[2]

Today, one easily sees in *Pitch*'s grand finale the last vestiges of that earliest and most hideous of racist images, the shuffling, big-eyed, black-faced comedian. In the dances of two old men, one sees the last flickerings of white America's predominant image of black America since the Civil War. What is hard to see, on first viewing, is the history behind these brief dances, the lives and roads that led these various performers to Greenville in the summer of 1947, where John Warner would document them on film.

Pitch captures in documentary fashion significant portions of the routines of Winstead's and Miller's shows. Those images, in and of themselves, are unique and priceless documents. Elsewhere we can find more famous black entertainers documented in their performances. We can even find routines from Miller and Lyles transferred verbatim from Broadway and vaudeville to film. (This Miller, Flournoy, was Irvin C.'s brother; together they represent two poles of marginalized, nearly buried, black entertainment forms. Miller and Lyles's *Shuffle Along*, some maintain, introduced the Harlem Renaissance to the nation. While Flournoy did Broadway and New York and then movies and Hollywood, Irvin C. ruled vaudeville and the road from 1915 until the form died, soon after *Pitch* was made.)

But never do the Hollywood film performances, even those in the best black cast films, show other performers from the same road show or depict the specific routines and costumes used during a season. Chorus routines may be similar, but they are slick. They lack what one sees in *Pitch* to such comic effect: the obligatory "stick" (or "white elephant"), the one character in every show who couldn't dance. It is partly the roughness of their performances, then, that is striking. What is never apparent is that long historical road that brought the art forms of vaudeville and minstrelsy together.

The mere conjoining of these two entertainment types in one film necessitates a quick foray into revisionist history. First, one needs to recognize that in almost every respect the terms "vaudeville" and "minstrelsy" cannot be discussed without racial designations. White and black vaudeville have distinctly different histories, but they at least share some similarities while white and black minstrelsy share virtually none. Vaudeville remains a generally acceptable entertainment form, though black vaudeville has not received the serious study it deserves. Minstrelsy is something else, even though, until its demise, black vaudeville and black minstrelsy offered basically the same formats and routines.

Both used blackfaced comics to the same minimal extent; that is, they both usually featured a comedy team, consisting of a straight man and a blackfaced comic, as one part of their shows. Yet minstrelsy carries with it a stigma, as though synonymous with "blackface," and thus with overt racism.

The image of minstrelsy, then, goes beyond the simple fact of men and women (usually no more than two out of a cast of fifteen to twenty) using charred cork as makeup or masking. Our contemporary image of minstrelsy derives largely from popular culture rather than history. First, there is the image which the term evokes for most people: an entire cast of whites in blackface doing racist jokes. In typically American fashion, we remember the origin mixed in with its perpetuation in white civic club and service organization fund-raisers staged across America well into the 1960s. But while it is true that the form was popularized in America by whites in blackface, they were originally doing antebellum plantation material, elaborate scenes and staged farces based more on white stereotypes than on any accurate rendering of the African-American experience in the South. Once black performers got into minstrelsy in a big way during the late 1870s, white performers moved on to vaudeville, taking with them their black face and attitudes, now transformed into the popular "coon" jokes and songs. These jokes, delivered in blackface, would survive in scripts peddled across the country and were later collected and rented out as "minstrel shows" in the same way that high school plays were distributed.

Meanwhile, the black performers, left with minstrelsy, began to change it into a form that was more their own, adding chorus routines, specialty acts, and grand finales. As blacks migrated from the rural South into northern urban centers, and particularly after Broadway was virtually closed to black performers around 1910, black vaudeville began to emerge. The vaudeville format soon spread to the tented minstrel shows. By the mid-1910s there was virtually no difference between black vaudeville and black minstrel shows other than management and venue.

During their day, neither vaudeville nor minstrel performers enjoyed respectable images, and stories of their wild behavior are legion. Yet that image, too, is unfair to minstrel shows like "Silas Green from New Orleans." Reports from their tours continually reflected how eagerly their visits were anticipated and how graciously they were received by

John Warner, in the doorway of his Plaza Theater, Greenville, North Carolina, where much of *Pitch* was filmed. (Courtesy of Shirley Warner Taylor)

local society and college communities. But by the 1930s, even the black press had begun to ignore them as the new generation frowned on their backward ways. Big bands and big venues became the measure of fame and success, and the New York scene was increasingly dominate.

Today, the reputation of black minstrel performers is complicated by misperceived images of the genre. Although in recent years a large number of biographies and autobiographies of black entertainers have appeared, few have dealt at all with the traveling minstrel shows. In some cases, the performers themselves deny their minstrel connections. Interviewers largely ignorant of this early form have no questions with which to prod their sources, and often when they hear for the first time names of "great" performers who are not documented elsewhere, it is easy to imagine that this information ultimately is ignored.

John Warner got his first camera in the early 1930s, and soon he was shooting newsreel footage for Pathe, as well as his own versions of home/community movies. These silents he would screen, unannounced,

Walter Warner, also known as William Lord. (Courtesy of Clyde Gallop)

Detail from a publicity still for "Brownskin Models", about 1935. (Courtesy of Katie Abraham)

with regular features at his Plaza Theater. It seemed logical, then, for him to move to movie production, but, always a dutiful father, he waited until his daughter graduated from college to form Lord-Warner Pictures. When the time came, he enlisted the aid of his brother, Walter, who had changed his name to William Lord in the 1920s, to write scripts and direct. Together, they became North Carolina's Warner Brothers. Some eastern North Carolina residents still refer to *Pitch* as "that movie Warner Brothers made."

John Warner knew the best local talent, and he had good connections with most of the traveling shows, with the result that he was able to hire for his film dynamic representatives of two of the most ignored forms of black entertainment in America. Those he hired were among the best still on the road.

Irvin C. Miller's "Brownskin Models" may well have been the most successful road show of all time. It began in New York about 1925 and toured regularly until about 1950. During the glory years of the Harlem Renaissance the show was mainly a northern urban attraction. In the 1930s, the show went on increasingly longer road tours through the South and to the West Coast. But the 1940s hit hard, and Miller found himself and his performers increasingly stranded, with busted plans and no money to pay the cast. On at least a few occasions he joined forces with "Winstead's Mighty Minstrels," and once or twice he teamed with the "Florida Blossoms Minstrels." Winstead had purchased title to one of Miller's 1920s revues, "Broadway Rastus," in the mid-1930s, and sometimes toured his second show under that name. Winstead, it seemed, was always around to bail out Miller and his performers when they were stranded.

"Winstead's Mighty Minstrels," on the other hand, was never more than a regional show. By the early 1930s, the tented minstrel show was confined almost exclusively to the South. While black vaudeville could still manage to attract city audiences, the minstrels were increasingly seen as throwbacks to an era most people preferred to forget. Little did it matter that the performers, and their routines, were virtually interchangeable with those of the vaudeville shows, which also were rapidly falling victim to movies, records, and radio.

Winstead left most of the show management to Frank Sloan, a circus and vaudeville veteran whom Winstead had befriended. Winstead's primary interests were always secondary to show business per se. Although he never paid performers well, he paid them regularly, and his shows never closed. He was also known as a soft touch, usually willing to pick up a stranded performer anywhere, whether or not the performer's act could be worked into the show. In reality, he needed the performers more than they needed him, for the show had to remain open so that Winstead and his partners, Wash Turner, Roscoe Grice, and Bill Payne, could carry on their real trades, which included running counterfeit money, stolen cars, and moonshine. During winter months, Winstead transferred his business to a neighborhood he developed in Fayetteville, stocked with chorus dancers-turned-prostitutes and gaming and drinking joints. During the traveling seasons he kept his performers on the road, working and regularly paid, while his show served essentially as a traveling hideout for his gang. (The gang fell apart in 1938 when Turner and Payne were arrested for the murder of an Asheville highway patrolman. They were subsequently executed in North Carolina's electric chair.)

By the time Winstead's show hit Greenville in 1947, Winstead himself was dead, and the show was under Sloan's management. Although it had lost most of its extracurricular income, it still claimed to be the best show on the road. It had, however, become more a haven of last resort for aging performers who had never cracked the New York–Hollywood scenes. And, ultimately, that is what makes "Winstead's Mighty Minstrels" performances in *Pitch a Boogie Woogie* so important.

Some might argue that these performers, because they did not record and only rarely made it onto the Apollo stage or into a Hollywood film, are therefore minor and worthy of little more than a footnote or two in the larger histories of American entertainment. But that is a limited perspective, based on contemporary notions of fame and that curious notion of New York somehow becoming the ultimate arbiter of a legitimate theatrical fame. In fact, many of the traveling performers avoided New York as surely as some of the big stars avoided the South. Stories were legion of performers falling prey to big city producers, of the Bessie Smiths and Fletcher Hendersons being exploited and then discarded. Winstead, in fact, was Bessie Smith's last employer, hiring her out of Philadelphia poverty in 1937 long after the meager sums she had earned from Columbia Records were depleted, even though the record company itself would long continue to make money off her songs. Our standard notions of fame easily ignore the ephemeral vaudeville and minstrel shows, which left no records of their performances but billboards, occasional local press notices, and indelible memories. For example, Princess White, long a star with "Silas Green from New Orleans," refused to give up her regular weekly pay for a shot at recording. Today, it seems that almost anyone who ever heard her sing claims she was superior to Bessie Smith, Ma Rainey, or Ida Cox.

The "Silas Green" show is the most enigmatic and probably the most important of the traveling minstrel shows. James Brown claims it as inspiration for his first revue. "That's what I tried to do," he says of his first road show. " 'Silas Green from New Orleans' was the best" (Brown and Tucker 1986:23). From 1902 to the beginning of World War II, it offered to black minstrelsy a counterpart to Miller's vaudeville reign. Yet, so little about it is known that scholars as noted as Paul Oliver (1969:58) erroneously refer to Silas Green's expert management and to its home base of New Orleans, when in fact Silas Green was but a fictional character in the show's running series of skits (played for the longest duration by Ford Wiggins), and it scarcely ever played New Orleans, much less based itself there. (During its first ownership years, it played out of Florida; from 1920 until it was absorbed into the James Strait carnival shows in the early 1950s, it was based in Georgia.)

After Charles Collier, its second owner, died in 1942, "Silas Green" suffered through the War years and afterward traveled in scaled-down versions for several years. Throughout most of the 1930s, its competition in the South was primarily "Winstead's Mighty Minstrels," and by virtue of maintaining a clean, family atmosphere, it never attracted the illegal monies that Winstead's show generated. As a result of the good reputation of "Silas Green," Winstead often hired its employees, offering them less money, perhaps, but a longer playing season, complete with room, board, and usually a place to stay in Fayetteville during the off-season. Rosters of the two shows are sometimes interchangeable. Invariably, when a performer changed shows, he took his or her own routines.

Winstead's show, begun in 1931, offers in *Pitch* some of that crossover, and much of the deep history of black tent, or minstrel, shows. Former performers who have seen *Pitch* all claim that its grand finale is nearly identical to its theatrical counterparts going back as far as 1917. Willie Earle was one of those aging greats, totally undocumented in contemporary history. Known as "The Georgia Preacher" for most of his career, Earle shows up in a brief dance routine in the grand finale

Willie Earle, in the grand finale of *Pitch*. (Still taken from the original 35mm nitrate by Patrick Keough)

Members of the original *Pitch* soundtrack band, the Rhythm Vets, at the film's 1987 re-premiere in Greenville, North Carolina. *Left to right,* Carl Foster, Charles Woods, Thomas Gavin, Lou Donaldson. The screening marked the first time the bandsmen had seen *Pitch*, and it was the first time they had played together since July 1947, when they recorded its soundtrack. (Photo by Tony Rumple, East Carolina University News Bureau)

of *Pitch*. In a career that ran from the mid-1910s to about 1950, Earle worked with Miller's "Brownskin Models," as well as with most of the major minstrel shows. In *Pitch*, he as well as the rest of the travelers with Winstead's and Miller's shows get no credit; were it not for the extraordinary recollections of a few key performers, they would all be unknown. As it is, several remain unknown but others are not: Willie "Ashcan" Jones, comedian and lindyhopper; the Count and Harriet, lindyhoppers; singers Sylvester "Tabu" Mike, Rosa Burrell, and Evelyn Whorton; chorus dancers Dorothy Lee, Catherine Johnson, and Teresa Jones.

None of these people saw *Pitch* in its original release. Some, since deceased, never will. Only a handful of the local performers ever had that chance, and for them *Pitch* quickly became but a memory. *Pitch* itself was nearly lost. John Warner abandoned his filmmaking career shortly after *Pitch*'s failure and went to work for a local television station. When he retired in the early 1960s, he purchased the Roxy Theater, built in 1948 across the street from the Plaza. At the Roxy, he would occasionally screen *Pitch*, always unannounced, with his regular fare. He died a broken man, with an estate worth barely eight hundred dollars, including an automobile. The surviving prints of *Pitch* were left, unclaimed, in the Roxy. Greenville musician Bill Shepherd discovered them around 1976, and finally, in 1986, the American Film Institute arranged for their restoration. Today, the restored 35mm print of *Pitch a Boogie Woogie* rests securely in the National Archives.

It was at *Pitch*'s 1987 re-premiere (and first screening for an integrated audience) that several of the cast, including most of the soundtrack musicians, saw it for the first time. Originally part of a dance band called "The Rhythm Vets," these musicians were all young Navy veterans and North Carolina A & T students and graduates, booked to provide the accompaniment to William Lord's five original songs. Therein lies one of the oddities of *Pitch*'s composition—the music was added after the songs had been sung and the dances danced. Saxophone player Thomas Gavin has likened it to playing music by the dance, instead of dancing to the music (Albright 1988).

But the Vets' inclusion on the soundtrack is important for more than technical reasons. They had all entered the navy as musicians, some to serve in Chapel Hill, North Carolina, in the navy's pre-flight training school, others to the famed Great Lakes Naval Base in Chicago where many of the top jazzmen of the 1950s got their musical training. When the war ended they all returned to Greensboro. Those from Chicago brought the fresh sound of bebop to mingle with the lingering strains of big band jazz favored by those who had stayed in North Carolina. The Vets' leader, Walter Carlson, has retired from his position as band director at North Carolina A & T University; most of the others, like Carlson, went into education, one of the few professions open to young blacks at the time. The notable exception was their star, Lou Donaldson, who made his professional recording debut on *Pitch*. He has recorded more than eighty jazz albums since leaving North Carolina for New York in 1950. To a man, the Vets saw nothing remarkable about their film work, most echoing Gavin's comment, "It was just another gig" (Albright 1988).

Pitch a Boogie Woogie's failure as a movie had more to do with national attitudes and local circumstances than it did with its cinematic problems. Today, it holds up well in comparison to most other race movies despite its wooden dialogue, slight script, and awkward cinematography. Still, sometimes it makes current audiences cringe with its strains of overt sexism, naive racism, and a notion that, because he was white, John Warner must have been, like other white promoters, exploiting his performers. None who worked for him shares that view.

The movie's timing and its composition offer telling metaphors for the way life was in 1948 in small southern towns still divided physically and philosophically along race lines. The entire history of race films parallels, in interesting ways, the history of race records, minstrelsy, and the various but consistent ways blacks have been treated by mainstream American popular culture. These, in turn, reflect our regional attempts at grappling with the questions and problems created by the separate-but-equal notions so long embraced by political leaders in America. Typically, the role African-Americans played in creating American popular culture has been downplayed or ignored, resulting in masked and simplified versions of the African-American experience. Early films like *Birth of a Nation* used whites in blackface to portray its villains, much as the early white minstrel shows used these same types to depict their happy plantation "darkies"; similarly, the first jazz recordings were by the white Original Dixie Land Jazz Band. Out of their first black minstrel shows, blacks began creating vaudeville-style routines, then music, and then films aimed at their own audiences. In-

Herman Forbes (*left*) and Tom Foreman before the dream begins.
(Still taken from original 35mm nitrate by Patrick Keough)

variably, when these audiences were seen as commercially exploitable, a white-controlled management intruded, took the form over, and transformed it into a safer, but blander, product. It happened to most of the black-cast minstrel shows, to race records, to race film, to popular dance, and even to rock and roll.

Interestingly, the parallels break down along one key difference: race films and vaudeville-styled minstrel shows never made the leap to white cultural acceptance, while records (and the music forms they introduced, as well as the dances they inspired) did. As a result, black musicians of the 1930s finally were able to capitalize to some extent on the successes of their predecessors in the twenties, who had virtually saved the recording industry once it realized that white consumers were anxious to pay for black jazz and blues. But black actors were continually relegated in the 1930s and 1940s to a few stereotypical roles in Hollywood, despite their starring roles in race films.

Two factors seem to have contributed separately, and ironically, to the race film industry's failure to be absorbed into a larger American cultural context while the race music industry evolved into the most dominant form of popular music in the world. (Of course, once again, by the time that happened, blacks were mostly excluded from commercial reward.) On one hand, the Jim Crow South created a ready market—hundreds of theaters where only black audiences went. Once those audiences sampled films with black casts, their appetite for more seems to have been insatiable. The demand was so great in the late 1920s that white production companies, except that of Oscar Micheaux, soon controlled the industry. They rode it out until its demise in 1948, even hastening it by cheap budgets and the notion of a captive, indiscriminating audience. Then, with the market identified and the stars becoming established, white cinema moved in to offer the biggest stars roles in its slicker productions. On the other hand, race music had infiltrated white homes via radio, word-of-mouth, and records, sneaking African-American artistry to white listeners who could, if they chose, forget about race while they listened. But with the movies, instead of intruding subtly into white perceptions, black faces loomed out of the darkness, larger than life, and there seems, at least in the minds of white Hollywood producers, too much of a memory of the terror of the madman rapist from *Birth of a Nation* to allow a black presence in any but the most stereotypical ways. (That image—of the white in blackface terrorizing the innocent white girl—makes an apt metaphor for the media's perpetuation of the exploitation of black Americans: a fear is articulated through stereotyping and the stereotype becomes the "reality," justifying continued exclusion.) And the move from this movie stereotype will persist through the successive characterizations of jazz, rhythm and blues, blues, rock and roll, and rap as sexually aggressive and threatening.

Musicians were the ones that most often escaped the stereotyping, though their escape itself would become a stereotype, the one nonthreatening, dignified way that blacks could portray themselves in film. (Notable exceptions abound: Louis Armstrong forced to don a tiger robe in the jungle motif of an early short; Bessie Smith crawling drunkenly on a barroom floor in *St. Louis Blues*.) As music evolved, it seems always it was the beginning of a new musical form that excited listeners the most, and it seems consistent that whites masked and then tamed early jazz into the charted, big band sounds of the 1930s. But no one could copy Charlie Parker's notes in the way Bennie Goodman had copied Fletcher Henderson's. The move into live rock-and-roll shows in the mid-1950s as the new cutting edge in entertainment only amplified the problem first suggested by white hipsters digging the underground sounds of bop, as Elvis was more marketable in person than Big Mama Thornton, Pat Boone more than Little Richard. And so, by the mid-1950s, most blacks in film and in music were nearly as close to the margins as they had been fifty years earlier.

Black vaudeville and minstrelsy spanned both the rise and fall of race records and cinema. It fostered their growth, nurtured the artists' careers, and entertained millions of black Americans during the years when the white world was closed to them. These traveling performers, more than the Mississippi River, the cities of New Orleans and Chicago, and the Great Migration, were responsible for spreading popular song and dance throughout the country. It wasn't until white-controlled media began disseminating them that the white world noticed. And now, historically, it seems to forget. But that denial can never completely cover them up, despite decades of distortion. The history of racial exploitation in America can be charted in the relationship of these shows to their audiences, for they were always there, as the other venues opened and closed according to white society's latest whims and fads. And in each succeeding stage it seems the white performer has been quick to jump on the fad and just as quick to nearly kill the substance beneath the fad—the original energy that led to the new form's emergence.

Beginning in the late nineteenth century, we witness white minstrels quickly vacating the minstrel stage once black performers were granted access to it. But white control of vaudeville, where the white performers went, kept blacks away. That did not stop black-cast productions in the early twentieth century from dominating much of early theater and popular culture. Blacks, then, developed their own vaudeville, and with no place to perform, soon had their own theaters and circuits to supply them. The music, like the dance and comedic routines, continued to evolve, culminating in the 1920s with such national crazes as jazz and the Charleston. Black vaudeville and minstrelsy enjoyed enormous successes throughout that decade, while white vaudeville fell quick victim to movies, surviving only through radio shows. But since the 1930s began, we have tended to view the history of blacks in entertainment solely through successes in New York and Chicago club scenes, recording contracts, and movie roles. In the process, we ignore the thousands of dance bands that took the vaudeville and minstrel stage to their next levels, where the audience became part of the show as it danced the Depression away.

Throughout all these separate but related evolutionary stages in American entertainment, only one—that of the black cast minstrel show—offered itself to integrated audiences. Before records and all through the years of segregated cinema, it offered the only glimpse most whites could ever get of a black community at work. Black vaudeville played to black audiences for the same reason race films did: the theaters were generally open only to those audiences. But the tent shows played on vacant lots wherever a deal could be struck, and in most of the small southern towns that supported the form long after most historians labelled it dead, towns too small in many cases to support even a single theater, it offered the only form of professional entertainment its residents could ever see. Lon Chaney, featured tapdancer in the Broadway hit *Black and Blue*, clearly recalls, "Silas Green was the first live music I ever saw—they were just marching down the middle of the street" (Chaney 1988). The minstrels paraded down Main Street, and people followed them en masse to the tent, where audiences were treated to a brief preview of the evening's entertainment. As a result, they attracted mixed audiences, though once inside the tent they'd likely be kept racially separate by ropes drawn through the center.

How much Burns and Allen, Jack Benny, and others appropriated from the comic routines presented in dance revues, and before them the minstrel and vaudeville stages, is as impossible to determine as who originally came up with the routine Pigmeat Markham popularized decades before "Laugh In" discovered it: "Here come da judge. . . ." Miller and Lyles's 1920s routines are filled with judge skits; they both got their training on the minstrel stages of the 1910s. The jokes, like the dances and the music, have had a fluid evolution we may never understand completely. But it seems clear that our best music did not always come out of recording studios; our best jokes did not require canned laughter; our best dances did not have to be taught by Arthur Murray schools; and countless of our best artistic performers were people whose stories we may never know. Why and how we gain access to what entertains us are questions that we seem just now to be asking. Our canonical thinking runs deep. It remains too easy, sometimes, to mistake the masked for the real.

Pitch a Boogie Woogie offers a window into all this: the end of the race film industry, black vaudeville, black minstrelsy, and big band jazz. It has a touch of the beginnings of bop, and to students of American dance it offers perhaps the only documentary-style performances of a distinct and extended stage in its development. It has unknown stars who will forever remain unknown. But it also carries the possibility that, one day, someone may be able to fill in Evelyn Whorton's history a little more or even identify Willie Earle's elderly dance partner. Their stories, all these stories, ultimately make *Pitch* a more important film than John Warner could ever have dreamed or than any of its stars, who labored for entire careers under the cloak of anonymity, would dare have imagined. Yet, *Pitch* can never be more than a small part of the vaster and infinitely more complicated history of how entertainment, and the industrialization of it, have shaped our nation.

NOTES

Much of this paper is based on surveys of several African-American newspapers, unpublished route and receipt books, and extensive interviews with *Pitch* cast members, Greenville residents, and former musicians, dancers, and vaudeville and minstrel performers. Invaluable background material on race films comes from Bogle (1974), Cripps (1977, 1978), Sampson (1980, 1988), Southern (1983), Stearns and Stearns (1968), Toll (1974), and Woll (1989).

1. Much of the information on vaudeville and black minstrel shows has been gleaned from surveys of the following black audience newspapers: Baltimore *Afro-American*, 1917–22; Chicago *Defender* (national editions), 1915–50; Indianapolis *Freeman*, 1899–1902, 1910–15; Norfolk *Journal-Guide*, 1916–17, 1921–25, 1937–42; and J. A. Jackson's entertainment page in *Billboard*, 1921–25. The Greenville *Reflector*, 1937–48, was also surveyed.

Pitch a Boogie Woogie is available in its entirety as part of the 1988 UNC-TV documentary *Boogie in Black and White*, which also features interviews with cast members and area residents.

2. Personal interviews were conducted with *Pitch* cast members Beatrice Atkinson, Robert Belcher, Herman Forbes, Willie Jones, Rev. Dr. Joe Little,

and sound track musicians Walter Carlson, Lou Donaldson, Richard Jones, Thomas Gavin, Jehovah Guy, Raymond Pettiford, and Charles Woods.

Personal interviews were also conducted with former musicians, dancers, and vaudeville and minstrel performers: Katie Bryant Abraham, Eleanor Baker, Peg Leg Bates, Olivette Miller Briggs, Lon Chaney, Ozell Joyner, J. L. Lowe, Sammy Lowe, Hortense Collier Sapp, Charlie Morrison, Birdie Johnson Rooks, Dicie Pettiford, James Powell, Dr. Milton Quigless, and William Robinson.

Greenville residents Filmore Bell, Pervis Cohen, E. H. Eaton, Mrs. Tom Foreman, Sr., Louise and Charles Shivers, and Sam Wooten also granted personal interviews. For further information, interested readers are encouraged to contact the author.

REFERENCES

ALBRIGHT, ALEX, 1988. *Boogie in Black and White*, Center for Public Television. WUNC, Chapel Hill, N.C., February 19.
BOGLE, DONALD, 1974. *Toms, Coons, Mulattoes, Mammies, and Bucks* (New York: Bantam).
BROWN, JAMES, and BRUCE TUCKER, 1986. *James Brown: The Godfather of Soul* (New York: Macmillan).
CHANEY, LON, 1989. Personal interview with the author. New York, N.Y., March 18.
CRIPPS, THOMAS, 1977. *Slow Fade to Black* (New York: Oxford University Press).
———, 1978. *Black Film as Genre* (Bloomington: Indiana University Press).
OLIVER, PAUL, 1969. *The Story of the Blues* (Philadelphia: Chilton).
SAMPSON, HENRY, 1980. *Blacks in Blackface* (Metuchen, N.J.: Scarecrow Press).
———, 1988. *The Ghost Walks* (Metuchen, N.J.: Scarecrow Press).
SOUTHERN, EILEEN, 1983. *The Music of Black Americans: A History*. 2nd ed. (New York: Norton).
STEARNS, MARSHALL, and JEAN STEARNS, 1968. *Jazz Dance: The Story of American Vernacular Dance* (New York: Macmillan).
TOLL, ROBERT C., 1974. *Blacking Up: The Minstrel Show in 19th Century America* (New York: Oxford).
WOLL, ALLEN, 1989. *Black Musical Theatre: From Coontown to Dreamgirls* (Baton Rouge: Louisiana State University Press).

PART 2
Opportunities from the Archives

Ordinary Life in the Southern Appalachians, 1925–1940: The Photographs of R. A. Romanes

Max E. White

With the close of World War I, soldiers from the United States returned home to resume their lives and vocations. For most of the returning veterans, life would change dramatically in the years ahead. Those veterans returning to the hill country of northeast Georgia and the western Carolinas would see dramatic change, too, but it came more slowly here. The scene to which they returned in 1918 or 1919 actually differed little from that of fifty or more years earlier, particularly in the countryside. Although a few individuals had purchased automobiles, the vast majority of people still traveled in wagons, in buggies, or on foot. Footpaths crisscrossed the countryside and supplemented the dirt roads as thoroughfares. Most of the arable land was cleared and was being farmed. Farming methods had changed little since white settlement of the area. Horses, mules, or steers were still being used throughout the area, and men, women, and children worked in the fields on the small family farms.

Since there was no electricity, there was no refrigeration, and milk and butter were often placed in the storm cellar to keep them cool during the summer months. Watermills still ground corn into meal, and in the lower part of the area cotton was still the cash crop. Farmers raised a few acres of cotton each year, and after picking, the cotton was hauled to the nearest gin. Other than the sale of milk, butter, eggs, and other farm products, cotton was virtually the only source of cash (other than illegal means, such as moonshining). People supplemented their garden produce by hunting and fishing. In some areas of the mountains the muzzle-loading rifle was still being used.

Crane House, Whiteside Cove, North Carolina, 1938. (Hunter Library, Western Carolina University; courtesy of Special Collections)

Farm scene near Yonah Mountain, White County, Georgia (undated). (Hunter Library, Western Carolina University; courtesy of Special Collections)

Max E. White

Cradling wheat near Alto, Georgia, 1938. (Hunter Library, Western Carolina University; courtesy of Special Collections)

In the uppermost Piedmont in northeast Georgia, peaches became a cash crop. Sold at roadside stands or shipped out via railroad, peaches were important to the local economy, for even children could earn money picking peaches or packing them for shipment.

It was into this scene that R. A. Romanes arrived in 1919. Reinfried Armstrong Romanes was born April 4, 1896, in Berlin. His father was a British citizen of Italian descent and his mother was German. At the outbreak of World War I, Reinfried and his father fled Germany (Reinfried's mother had died several years earlier). Returning to England, Reinfried joined the Royal Scottish Fusileers, and because of his fluency in both English and German, he served as an intelligence agent (Scull 1985:231). After the war he worked in a nursery while studying horticulture. Desiring to spend some time in America, he contacted the British Consulate General in Georgia, who arranged for him to visit, and he was temporarily housed with the family of Clement Cornwall, a British-American citizen in Alto, Georgia. Here he began working, eventually becoming foreman in the Cornwalls' apple and peach orchards. He extended his visa and was to remain in Alto for the rest of

Sherman Wade tying a sheaf of wheat near Alto, Georgia (undated). (Hunter Library, Western Carolina University; courtesy of Special Collections)

Boys working in a peach orchard near Alto, Georgia, 1930s. (Hunter Library, Western Carolina University; courtesy of Special Collections)

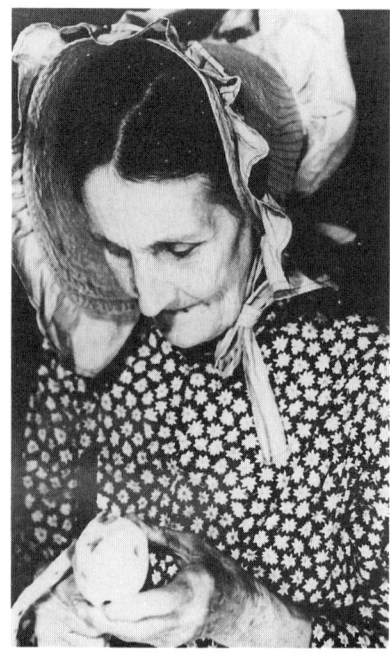

Left: Wildy Payne peeling potatoes, 1939. (Hunter Library, Western Carolina University; courtesy of Special Collections)

Below, left: Sherman Wade posing with a wheat cradle near Alto, Georgia (undated). (Hunter Library, Western Carolina University; courtesy of Special Collections)

Below, right: Walt Cook picking peaches near Alto, Georgia, 1936. (Hunter Library, Western Carolina University; courtesy of Special Collections)

his life. Possessing an inquisitive mind, he pursued a number of interests, including mathematics, horticulture, ornithology, and, beginning about 1925, photography.

Known to locals simply as Romanes, he began documenting a way of life that was even then changing rapidly. Although he photographed a wide range of subjects (birds, especially purple martins, trains, landscapes), his photographs of the people of the region capture the viewer like none of his other works. Romanes photographed some people as they worked, and posed others; the results are evocative images of a rural population in a changing era, of people retaining old ways (which were all they had known for generations), yet being caught up in the inevitable, suffering through the Depression, being drawn ever more rapidly into the modern world with its industries, materialism, and new life styles. Here we see the elderly, reluctant to give up the old ways; the young, eager and enthusiastic, knowing some of the traditional ways, yet willingly accepting the new.

Romanes documented the end of an era and the beginning of another. Most of his photographs were taken in Banks, Habersham, White, Rabun, and Stephens counties in northeast Georgia and in adjacent counties in North Carolina and South Carolina. Going about in the company of one or two friends from the community, he traveled to Gainesville, Georgia, to photograph the destruction of the tornado of April 6, 1936, during which more than two hundred people were killed. He photographed local towns strung out along the tracks of the Southern Railroad, towns like Cornelia and Lula. Many of his photos are of the steam locomotives on the Southern Railroad. Some of his works appeared in the magazine section of the Atlanta *Journal and Constitution* Sunday edition.

The photographs of Romanes go beyond mere nostalgia. They capture the region of the upper Piedmont and Southern Appalachians in a period of profound change. The people of the region were being pulled into events of the larger world. The agricultural way of life, based on the small family farm, was disappearing. Much of the land, which is cleared and either in pasture or in cultivation in his photos, would soon revert to scrub growth and woodland. Today, farming has all but ceased. Few people even have gardens. Romanes captured on film activities that had survived into the twentieth century in a rather isolated part of the South. Here are photographs of men cradling wheat, plowing with mules, and driving oxen. Other photos show timeless activities: a woman peeling potatoes, a girl churning while tending a baby. One photo is of a Confederate veteran cleaning his favorite rifle. This is a unique collection of photos, for at a time when family photographs recorded people in their Sunday-best clothing, Romanes captured everyday activities. Those activities were not regarded as unique or unusual at the time, but now are seen as documents of a way of life that once was, but is no more. R. A. Romanes was unique because he was a photographer of the ordinary as well as the extraordinary.

Perhaps his photographic talent was colored in part by his German-Scottish background, for life in the hill country of Georgia and the Carolinas would not have been "ordinary" to him. In some ways, the Romanes photographs are reminiscent of other photographic works of the period, for works of photographers like Eudora Welty (1989) often depict people, small towns, and local stores in the South. But Romanes seems to have captured something else in his photographs. In a manner not seen in the works of photographers of the Depression era like Walker Evans and Dorothea Lang, Romanes captures the spirit of the people. His photographs are often rather lighthearted and do not focus on the forlorn images of the destitute. Most of his subjects were friends, neighbors, or acquaintances who willingly allowed him to photograph them as they went about their daily tasks. The overall theme that seems to speak through his photographs of mountain life is that "life is tough, but we will survive."

At his death in 1978, Romanes's photograph collection was inherited by William Shore, grandson of Clement Cornwall. Through Shore's efforts the photographs of Romanes have been the subject of a special exhibit at the Mountain Heritage Center at Western Carolina University in Cullowhee, North Carolina. Subsequently, several of the photographs, along with a biographical sketch of Romanes, were published in *Foxfire* magazine and in a *Foxfire* calendar. The entire collection is now housed in the Special Collections section of Hunter Library at Western Carolina University. It is with the cooperation of Mr. William Shore, the staff at *Foxfire*, and Hunter Library, Western Carolina University, that these photos were made available. Anyone interested in the documentary history of the study area will find a rich source of material in the R. A. Romanes collection.

NOTE

The Romanes photos in this presentation are used with the permission of William A. Shore, the staff at *Foxfire*, and the staff in the Special Collections Section, Hunter Library, Western Carolina University, Cullowhee, North Carolina.

REFERENCES

SCULL, HEATHER, 1985. R.A.R. Photography Collection . . . The Images of a Fading Era. *Foxfire* 19:230–41.
WELTY, EUDORA, 1989. *Eudora Welty Photographs* (Jackson: University Press of Mississippi).

Constructing the Florida Seminole on Film, 1850–1950

Patsy West

This essay provides a historical survey of the photographic record of the Florida Seminole between 1850 and 1950 and reviews the work of a number of photographers who have made notable contributions to the photographic record. Because the Seminole were reluctant to have their camps photographed, most of the photographs are portraits rather than images that depict Seminole culture. The rich anthropological literature on the cultural patterns of the Florida Seminole (MacCauley 1883; Skinner 1913; Spoehr 1941; Sturtevant 1971) is complemented by this remarkable photographic record that is primarily the result of nonacademic efforts.

The first known photographs of the Seminole were taken shortly before the outbreak of the Third Seminole War, during a historic tour of New York in 1852 by a Seminole delegation. The federal emigration division took the head chief, Billy Bowlegs, and his delegation from Tampa to New York, where they were wined and dined in hopes of persuading them to lead the survivors of the Second Seminole War, an estimated 450 persons, west to Indian territory in Oklahoma (Covington 1981:19). That plan turned out to be futile, but the trip did result in a fine photographic study of the resplendent Seminole leader at the popular Meade Brothers Broadway studio (Holmes 1990:7).

In all, the Seminole fought three wars with the United States between 1818 and 1858 while attempting to establish their right to remain in Florida. In the end they failed, and Bowlegs was again photographed during his emigration to Oklahoma in 1858. The last postwar emigrations of Florida Seminole took place in 1859. The two hundred or so Seminole who were left in the state following the third, and last, Seminole war understandably avoided contact with outsiders. No images of Florida Seminole have been documented between 1858 and 1870, a period of isolation in the cultural history of the Florida Seminole (Sturtevant 1971:111).

The earliest postwar photographs were made in the 1870s, when the Seminole journeyed to coastal frontier settlements, visiting lighthouses and beachside aid stations erected for shipwreck survivors. At trading posts the Seminole exchanged deerskins, otter pelts, alligator hides, and bird plumes destined for an international market.

Ralph M. Munroe was a prominent pioneer in Miami's Coconut Grove and was the area's most capable photographer. The Seminole were intriguing subjects for him, but he experienced major difficulties in his early efforts to photograph them in the 1870s and 1880s. He was finally able to coax some young men into having their photographs taken, giving each a print of himself; however, he was not allowed near the Seminole camp, nor near the women. Munroe attempted to photograph the women when the Indians broke camp and were ready to embark in their canoes, but the women lay down in the bottom of the canoes and covered themselves with blankets (Rockwood 1891:687). The Kirk Munroes, authors and neighbors of photographer Munroe, had a similar experience in the 1890s. Mary Barr Munroe (1909) recalled, "We were sailing up the Miami River, and met old Mattlo [now dead and the last of the war chiefs] and his two squaws poling a canoe. Of course, we tried to photograph them, but before my husband could get the camera set [it was before Kodak days] the two squaws threw themselves face down in the canoe and turned their skirts over their heads."

Women were, in fact, seldom photographed before the 1890s. They commanded special respect in the matrilineal culture and chose to have little contact with non-Indians. A handwritten note on the reverse of one photograph (now in a Michigan collection) read: "[Bowlegs] was asked to bring his squaw in and have his picture taken but he flatly refused saying, 'No—Squaw—she die!' After much persuasion and the promise of a dollar the chief finally posed for his photo" (Pohrt Collection 1983).

An article on the Florida Seminole by Caroline Rockwood appeared in *Leslie's Popular Monthly*, December 1891, illustrated by Ralph Munroe. Rockwood (1891:675) noted: "Of course my desire to obtain photographs of these and all Seminoles that I saw was intense, and in some cases was easily gratified, for [Munroe] was both ready and equal to the occasion, if the subject could be caught!" Yet, while some photos were easily obtainable, most were "the result of untiring effort and in some cases duplicity and effrontery possible only under just such circumstances."

The few existing Munroe photographs of Seminole subjects are rich in portraiture. Apparently his Indian subjects became more responsive to his camera, as all of the existing portraits are classically posed individuals and groups. The lack of women perhaps shows that they continued to demur. According to biographer Arva Moore Parks (1977:154) Munroe took photographs of the Seminole "in their Everglades homes, but unfortunately none of these pictures have survived."

At the home of William Freeman, my great-grandfather, on Little River several miles north of Munroe's house, the young photographer Otto Sonstebo, a Norwegian immigrant, took a number of photographs of Seminole who camped on our family property in 1893. Family oral history notes that the Indians were originally so apprehensive of having their pictures taken that my great aunt often stood in the back row with them, ducking out of sight at the last moment (E. M. West 1974). The few remaining Seminole portraits in the Sonstebo collection, however, show the Seminole assuming relaxed poses.

As towns grew in frontier south Florida around the turn of the century, photographic studios opened in Fort Myers, Bartow, Fort Pierce, Palm Beach, and Miami. Most frequently it was the Seminole men coming to town on trading business who succumbed to the studio photographer and his tip money. Often the men had made purchases of hats, vests, trousers, or shoes, and they often posed wearing their new purchases. Doubtless they wished to document their new finery, as the Seminole elders at this time generally disapproved of such untraditional accessories and forbade the young men to wear them in camp (Cory 1896:21).

In the remote trading area of Everglade near the Ten Thousand Islands in southwest Florida, young Bruce Storter was in charge of aiding tourists who wished to take photographs of the Seminole who traded at his father's store. Sometimes, they required bribing with "cheap cigars and bits of tobacco" (Kersey 1975:111).

The photographs, which depict more than just portraiture in the latter nineteenth and early twentieth centuries, come from those photographers who, from repeated trips, were familiar with both the Everglades and its Seminole inhabitants. One such person was Field Museum orni-

Patsy West

Vests, bowler hats, and watch fobs were important items of trade for the men in this 1904 postcard, while the women (who were financially independent) were content with such traditional finery as beads and cloth. The women cover their exposed midriffs by crossing their arms. By the next decade, the ruffle on the blouse was gradually extended to cover the exposed waist and eventually became a separate cape reaching to the wrists. (Seminole/ Miccosukee Photo Archive, no. 1218)

thologist Charles Barney Cory. Cory collected from the 1870s to the late 1890s. He was fascinated with the Seminole and became close to a number of the men such as Robert Osceola, who named his young son (a future tribal leader) for the scientist. Cory's existing photographs feature a number of women. Some are even smiling, probably attesting to his familiarity with their families over the years.

In his publication *Hunting and Fishing in Florida*, C. B. Cory included some of the most valuable nineteenth-century information on Seminole lifestyle and hunting techniques, illustrated with photographs. Around 1895, he photographed a manatee hunt on New River in what is now downtown Fort Lauderdale, providing the only known documentation of this important hunting technique. The manatee was harpooned and dove underwater. The detachable harpoon had a buoy attached that showed where the manatee was hiding. When the manatee surfaced for air, it was shot, towed to shore, and butchered (Cory 1896:25).

H. A. Ernst of Youngstown, Ohio, visited the New River area in the latter 1890s. Ernst's photographs depict major Seminole families such as the Charlie Willies who frequented the Stranahan Trading Post. Most notable in his collection, however, are the only known photos made at the Seminole's most historic site, the postwar settlement of Pine Island, located in the Everglades several miles west of Fort Lauderdale. These photographs proved valuable in the preservation of this unique two-and-one-half-mile-long island that was dedicated as the Seminole's first historic site in 1990. At the time of Ernst's visit, the Pine Island complex served as one of the last attempts to hold the reduced postwar Seminole population in their traditional town system of clan camps with a ceremonial ground (West 1989a).

As late as 1910, Alanson Skinner (1913:63 and 1918:37–38) noted a strong avoidance of non-Indians during his exploratory and material culture collecting expedition for the American Museum of Natural History in the Big Cypress. Even with non-Indian and Indian guides who were familiar with the Indian communities, his expedition was refused access to an important island community. The elderly leader of this community stated that it was all right for the guide to come to his camp. He was well known, but, "Don't bring another white man with you!"

However, it was probably the Everglades environment itself that was the greatest deterrent to ethnographic photodocumentation of the Seminole on their homeground. The inaccessibility of their settlements in the unsurveyed Everglades kept out all but the most adventuresome. Skinner was fortunate to have as his photographer Julian A. Dimmock, who had earlier explored the Everglades and, with the help of his father, writer Anthony W. Dimmock, established good relationships with the Seminole. The Dimmocks' adventures had taken them through the Everglades in canoes and ox carts.

The Dimmocks' ventures were not without mishap. Once while crossing an Everglades prairie, their ox cart was struck by lightning: "The team ran away, the boy who was driving was knocked down and I felt like a live wire" (Dimmock and Dimmock 1908:243). In another season, Anthony (1908:233, 240) related, "The water shoaled until we could hardly budge the canoes. Then came the weary days of hauling the canoes through soft, sticky mud. We followed trails in the Glades until they dried into mud paths."

Anthony Dimmock's writings, and Munroe's as well, relate how difficult it was to make photographs of the Seminole. Dimmock also revealed the photographers' difficulty in gaining access to all areas of interest in the Seminole camps. Once, they arrived at Tommy Osceola's camp and found the family away on a hunt. He noted (1908:238), "We kept house in Osceola's camp for a day, to give the cameraman an inning, as he claimed that the absence of the family afforded unusual opportunities to one of his profession."

Julian Dimmock's photographs reveal daily activities in the Big Cypress Interior: visits to the trading post at the head of Everglade navigation; canoeing; fishing; the island camps; boat landings; work areas; and such camp tasks as food preparation and silvermaking. He also documented the Big Cypress men dressed in their hunting gear and in festive attire.

Because of the Seminole's isolated state, many of their cultural ways remained unchanged well into this century. It was therefore possible to photographically document some traditions that had been noted in the earlier literature. Julian Dimmock's photographs are valuable for their documentation of Seminole cultural traditions.

Since the wars of the nineteenth century, the Seminole elders had been concerned about white knowledge of Seminole culture. It would seem that their reservations about photographic documentation of their camps was a result of their fear of being forcibly removed from Florida. They felt that the whites were much too curious, which could somehow do them harm. Mary Barr Munroe (1909) observed, "They used to dislike to be photographed, and would take to the woods or do almost anything to prevent it, but this objection is easily overcome now by paying for the privilege." Special Agent Lorenzo D. Creel took Kodak portraits of Seminole in the Fort Lauderdale area on a trip in 1911. Upon his return, he gave the prints to the Indians and noted (1911:19), "They seemed much pleased. . . ." In reviewing the photographs illustrating this era of trade, we find that they are limited primarily to physical appearances, architecture, and canoeing scenes. Numerous images in towns and on major rivers near the trading posts underscore the all-important trading economy.

The Dimmock photographs were made at the end of an era, as the Everglades drainage program, with its attendant investors and real estate agents, made its impact on south Florida. The success of the drainage program gradually began to extinguish Seminole traditions, which were based on the Indians' complete utilization of their environment.

During the 1920s, Claude C. Matlack, a well-known Miami society photographer, showed a great interest in the local Seminole. His photo sequence of Seminole dugouts on the Tamiami Canal in 1921 was one of the last to record the wide-scale usage of this means of transportation. Due to Everglades drainage operations, the dugout became obsolete in key areas, curtailing the hunting economy and seasonal gathering and visiting. In some areas, Seminole families began to pick vegetables for white farmers, who often utilized the rich island hummocks that had been the sites of Seminole camps and gardens before drainage and were accessible only by canoe. The Seminole were forced off as the newly accessible real estate was sold (West 1985:9).

In 1917 two tourist attractions featuring Seminole Indian villages were opened on the Miami River. Their success created other such enterprises. Although these commercial settings were criticized as being detrimental to the well-being of the Seminole, the Seminole themselves found the attractions to be suitable havens where they could make a living after the cataclysmic changes brought about by drainage and development (West 1981). At these riverside attractions, tourists took thousands of snapshots while some professional photographers made extensive use of these "city" Seminole villages.

At the tourist attractions, the Indians were presented as themselves, "Florida Seminole Indians," whose lifestyle and colorful patchwork clothing was of great interest to tourists of south Florida. The Seminoles came and went at will. They cooked traditional foods, lived in a typical camp of thatched chickees, sewed clothing, cared for children, and generally went about their daily tasks, becoming immune to the tourists' stares. Occasionally they posed for photographs for which they were tipped (West 1981).

Matlack's tourist attraction photographs from the 1920s were used to illustrate ethnomusicologist Francis Densmore's Bureau of American Ethnology publication *Seminole Music* (1956). The photographs of Frank A. Robenson, who was in charge of a large department store and photographic salon in Miami, were taken at the Musa Isle tourist attrac-

Children living in Miami's largest Seminole Indian tourist attraction, Musa Isle, pose with an alligator prop in the early 1930s. Their fathers often wrestled live alligators at the attraction, where the families lived during the six-month tourist season. (Photo by R. R. Doubleday, Seminole/Miccosukee Photo Archive, no. 1215B)

tion. Florence I. Randle's studies of Musa Isle Seminole produced for the Work Projects Administration in 1937 were used to illustrate *Seminole Indians in Florida*. Published in 1941, this state agricultural bulletin was the major popular work available on the Florida Seminole for many years (Writers Program 1941).

Despite the commercialization of the tourist attractions, the reconstructed villages were often occupied by some of the most traditional families who maintained traditional patterns of tribal life. Families departed and returned from hunting trips in the Everglades; customs of food preparation and hygiene were observed; canoes were hewn and repaired; babies were born in secluded areas near the camps; and canoe-making, alligator hunting, fishing, gathering "coontie" (a starch plant), and the making of clothing and basketry were ongoing activities (West 1981). In retrospect, it is unfortunate that these very accessible city attractions were not utilized more fully by ethnographers.

An isolated incident that took place at Musa Isle illustrates a breakdown in the Seminole's tourist attraction economics involving photo-

One of the many postcards published by R. R. Doubleday in the 1930s depicts Jane Tiger Motlow sewing patchwork clothing on a hand-cranked sewing machine in a temporary camp (identifiable as such by the canvas tarpaulin, rather than palmetto-thatch, shelter). This photo shows the versatile Singer sewing machine that enabled the Seminole to produce their unique patchwork clothing while living in distant settlements or in the tourist attractions of Miami. (Seminole/Miccosukee Photo Archive, no. 884)

graphic representation of the Seminole. Since the 1920s, the Seminole had been persuaded with salary, food, and craft supplies to live seasonally in the attractions, but by the late 1940s some families had become so wedded to tourist income that they lived in the tourist villages year-round and thus became more vulnerable to unscrupulous managers.

In correspondence dated March 1946, between an outraged tourist and O. B. White, a local attorney who frequently handled Seminole legal cases, the tourist described "one of the most brutal beatings I ever hope to see," witnessed by herself and one hundred tour-boat excursion passengers at one of Miami's Seminole villages. The letter included a graphic description of a mother's beating of her five-year-old daughter. White found upon investigation that "this child had been violating one of the requirements of the Indians, which is a matter of great necessity to them, in that the child had permitted visitors to take her picture without first obtaining some 'money' therefor, and when one understands that this 'money' frequently supplies food and often means the difference between luxury and denial, as these people receive nominal rations in these camps, then you can realize the gravity of this situation to this child's mother" (White 1946). It was customary in these attractions to give the Seminole tip money for posing for photographs.

W. Stanley Hanson, a native of Fort Myers, Florida, learned "Mikasuki" (Hitchiti), the language of the majority of the Florida Indians, at an early age as a result of his family's friendship with the Big Cypress band of Indians who came into Fort Myers to trade. His lifelong involvement created a statewide charitable group, the Seminole Indian Association, which under his guidance promoted and aided the Florida Seminole from 1913 to 1945. His participation in important Seminole councils gained him the title "White Medicine Man." Through his efforts a sizeable number of Seminole moved onto the Big Cypress Reservation for the first time (West 1990). Portraits abound in the remnants of Hanson's photo collection. Because of his close contact with the Big Cypress Seminole, smiles are the norm. It can also be seen that he was careful to record cultural activities in the isolated Big Cypress camps which he felt illustrated Seminole lifestyle.

The journalist and photographer Charles Ebbets worked for the *Miami News*. In 1934 the *News* ran a series by Cecil R. Warren that was conceived to alert the public to the ever increasing Seminole welfare needs on and off the reservations. The series was illustrated by Ebbets. Out for a story, Ebbets supposedly photographed a Mikasuki Green Corn Dance in 1938, an event in which uninvited non-Indian visitors are still unwelcome. While Ebbets's photographs truly depict various aspects of the day and nighttime activities, the participants are only one extended family and not a tribal gathering. It would appear that Ebbets persuaded the family to stage a mock Corn Dance for his photo session. While the event may have been trumped up, the photographs of activities appear accurate, making Ebbets's efforts of some value to the photographic record.

Even Louis Capron (1953), who published on the Seminole Green Corn Dance in a *Bureau of American Ethnology* bulletin, did not photograph the proceedings of the ceremonials, although he was a welcomed guest. He photographed the Muscogean Seminole's Corn Dance and Hunting Dance Grounds from an extreme distance, apparently on the sly. The schoolteacher-photographer William Boehmer, whose in-depth

Deaconess Harriet M. Bedell, Annie Charlie, and children in the Everglades. This photo is by the earliest identified Seminole photographer, Frank Charlie, who was Deaconess Bedell's driver. Circa 1935. (Seminole/Miccosukee Photo Archive, no. 1137)

photographic endeavors will be discussed, apparently never even took his camera to the Corn Dance, knowing that he was not welcome to document this festival (Boehmer and Boehmer 1990).

Gleason W. Romer, like Ebbets, worked for the *Miami News* and is credited for his superb documentation of the city of Miami. Seminole were frequently in the news and were paid to "add color" to city openings and other events. Romer, for example, chronicled the first airborne Seminole in the dirigible *Defender* in 1929 and Seminole registering to vote in 1931.

In 1933, the Episcopal deaconess Harriet M. Bedell traveled from Alaska to south Florida, where she began her twenty-seven-year mission to the Seminole from her base at Everglade City. She was a prolific snapshot photographer, as was her frequent driver, the Mikasuki Seminole Frank Charlie. Her photographs document the Seminole families who came to Glade Cross Mission to sell goods at her craft cooperative

Laura and Randolph Clay rock their newborn brother, Dwight Ike, in a traditional hammock in their new wooden home on the Brighton Reservation in 1956. The photographer was William D. Boehmer, instructor at the Brighton Day School. (Seminole/Miccosukee Photo Archive, Boehmer Collection, no. 201-1)

and the Seminole camps she frequently visited along the Tamiami Trail and Big Cypress Interior (West 1984).

In 1938, William and Edith Boehmer came to Florida from a teaching assignment among the Sioux of Lake Wapamini, South Dakota. Boehmer had been an avid photographer since his youth in Missouri. For the next twenty-seven years, he photographed the Seminole on the Brighton Reservation near Lake Okeechobee. Initially the students did not speak

Seeking higher education, Connie Frank left the security of her home camp with her aunt Jane Tiger Motlow to attend Haskell Institute Indian Boarding School in Lawrence, Kansas. (Photo by William D. Boehmer, Okeechobee, Florida, September 1956. Seminole/Miccosukee Photo Archive, Boehmer Collection, no. 236-1)

English, and they ran from the Boehmers. But soon the school and the Boehmers became the focal point of the reservation.

Although Boehmer's camera may have initially been a source of irritation to the Seminole, they became used to it and came to respect the man behind it. But it was not until Boehmer gave his negatives to the Smithsonian in the 1970s and gave copies to the Seminole Tribe that the Seminole people realized how thoroughly he had documented their lives. They never thought about it as he was snapping pictures through the years.

Boehmer attended every event: when the students left their traditional families to go away to boarding school; when they graduated from local high school; when they went to the prom in their first fancy clothes; when they attended teas, took trips to the shoe store, and received visits from the doctor. While he photographed the events that heralded change, he also documented traditional ways, such as a medicine man holding turkey quill scarifiers for the Green Corn Dance, or the time-consuming job of nailing palm fronds for thatching a chickee, or a woman shelling beans on a traditional log platform.

In 1941 Edith Boehmer began the Seminole Craft Cooperative. This had a great impact on the Florida Seminole, creating arts and crafts markets and improving the quality of the crafts being produced. Meanwhile Boehmer traveled through the reservation documenting housing, cattle barons, teenagers, the first Seminole service men, and the first nontraditional weddings. He also chronicled the important tribal organizational meetings in the latter 1950s and the first elected officers of the newly chartered Seminole Tribe of Florida.

The Boehmers both passed away in 1990 at the age of eighty-five. As teachers of reading, mathematics, and various "civilizing" skills, they had been the mentors to many Seminole Tribal members. The Boehmers' photographs are intimate and document the progress of these very adaptive people as they emerged into the modern world outside the reservation with the knowledge and confidence given to them by the Boehmers (Boehmer and Boehmer 1990; Billie 1990; Shore 1990).

Today, the tribal leaders have created a profitable position in the marketplace, in high-stakes bingo, tax-free smoke shops, and the new citrus industry. They have the legal savvy and finances to maintain such an empire. Adapting to new situations while maintaining their tribal identity appears to be what the Seminole do best.

NOTE

The Seminole/Miccosukee Photographic Archive, Fort Lauderdale, Florida, was begun as a research collection in 1972. It contains more than ten thousand photographic images taken from 1852 to the present. While the work of more than sixty photographers has been identified, the archive's major photographic holdings are those of W. Stanley Hanson, 1913–45, 532 images; William D. Boehmer, 1938–70, 5,000 images; and Henry Moretti, 1965–70, 1,135 images. The archive collects and documents photographs, archival materials, and ethnographic specimens.

This private archive is used by the Seminole Tribe of Florida, the Miccosukee Tribe of Indians of Florida, historical associations, museums, the media, and Indian families. Since 1986 the archive has contributed an award-winning historical series "Reflections" to the *Seminole Tribune* newspaper, Seminole Tribe of Florida. In 1990 the archive cosponsored "Patchwork and Palmettos," the first symposium to be held on Seminole/Miccosukee folk arts.

REFERENCES

BILLIE, JAMES E., 1990. Edith Boehmer Memorial Service, July 21, Mount Dora, Fla.; William D. Boehmer Memorial Service, December 1, Mount Dora, Fla.

BOEHMER, WILLIAM DYER, and EDITH M. BOEHMER, 1990. Videotaped interviews with the author. March 13 and September 8; Boehmer Papers on file at the Seminole/Miccosukee Photographic Archive, Fort Lauderdale, Fla.

CAPRON, LOUIS, 1953. The Medicine Bundles of the Florida Seminole and the Green Corn Dance. Bureau of American Ethnology Bulletin 151 (Washington, D.C.: Government Printing Office), pp. 155–210.

CORY, CHARLES BARNEY, 1896. *Hunting and Fishing in Florida*, 2nd ed. (Boston: Estes and Lauriat).

COVINGTON, JAMES W., 1981. *The Billy Bowlegs War, 1855–1858: The Final Stand of the Seminoles Against the Whites* (Chuluota, Fla.: Mickler House Publishers).

CREEL, LORENZO D., 1911. *Report of Investigation of the Seminole Indians in Florida to Commissioner of Indian Affairs from Special Agent, Washington*. Transcript in files of the Seminole/Miccosukee Photographic Archive, Fort Lauderdale, Fla.

DENSMORE, FRANCES, 1956. *Seminole Music*. Bureau of American Ethnology Bulletin 161 (Washington, D.C.: Government Printing Office).

DIMMOCK, ANTHONY W., and JULIAN A. DIMMOCK, 1908. *Florida Enchantments* (New York: Outing Publishing Company).

HOLMES, JACK D. L., 1990. A Florida Tourist in Gotham: Billy Bowlegs and

His 1852 Visit to New York City. Paper presented at the annual meeting of the Florida Historical Society, Tampa.
KERSEY, HARRY A., JR., 1975. *Pelts, Plumes, and Hides: White Traders among the Seminole Indians, 1870–1930* (Gainesville: University Presses of Florida).
MACCAULEY, CLAY, 1883. The Seminole Indians of Florida. Fifth Annual Report of the Bureau of Ethnology (Washington, D.C.: Government Printing Office), pp. 469–531.
MUNROE, MRS. KIRK (MARY BARR), 1909. Seminole Indian Women. *Jacksonville Times Union*, June 6.
PARKS, ARVA MOORE, 1977. *The Forgotten Frontier: Florida Through the Lens of Ralph Middleton Munroe* (Miami: Historical Association of Southern Florida).
POHRT, RICHARD SR., 1983. Data on photograph, Flint, Mich. Private collection.
ROCKWOOD, CAROLINE WASHBURN, 1891. Seminoles at Home. *Leslie's Popular Monthly* 32:643–86.
SHORE, JIM, 1990. Edith Boehmer Memorial Service, July 21, Mt. Dora, Fla.
SKINNER, ALANSON A., 1913. Notes on the Florida Seminole. *American Anthropologist* 15:63–77.
———, 1918. Ingraham Charlie, My Friend All'E Time. *American Indian Magazine* 6:36–39. Reprinted in 1987 in *A Seminole Sourcebook*, William C. Sturtevant, ed. (New York: Garland), pp. 36–39.
SPOEHR, ALEXANDER, 1941. Camp, Clan, and Kin among the Cow Creek Seminoles of Florida. Anthropological Series, 33 (Chicago: Field Museum of Natural History), pp. 1–27.
STURTEVANT, WILLIAM C., 1971. Creek into Seminole. In *North American Indians in Historical Perspective*, Eleanor B. Leacock and Nancy O. Lurie, eds. (New York, Random House), pp. 92–128.
WARREN, R. CECIL, 1934. *Florida's Seminoles* (Miami: Stirling Press).
WEST, ETHEL M., 1974. Interview with author, Fort Lauderdale, Fla. Seminole/Miccosukee Photographic Archive, Fort Lauderdale, Fla.
WEST, PATSY, 1981. The Miami Indian Tourist Attractions: A History and Analysis of a Transitional Mikasuki Seminole Environment. *Florida Anthropologist* 34:200–24.
———, 1984. Glade Cross Mission: An Influence on Florida Seminole Arts and Crafts. *American Indian Art* 9:58–68.
———, 1985. Seminoles in Broward County: The Pine Island Legacy. *New River News* (Fort Lauderdale Historical Society), 23:4–11.
———, 1989a. Seminole Indian Settlements at Pine Island, Broward County, Florida: An Overview. *Florida Anthropologist* 42:43–56.

——, 1989b. The Seminole of the Big Cypress Swamp: A Historical Survey. *Florida Anthropologist* 42:240–48.

WHITE, O. B., 1946. Letter on file. Seminole/Miccosukee Photographic Archive, Fort Lauderdale, Fla.

WRITERS PROGRAM (Florida), 1941. *Seminole Indians in Florida*. (Tallahassee: Florida State Department of Agriculture).

Moving Images of the Filmic South: Mining the WSB Television Collection

John Edgar Reid, Jr.

No where is the use of visual imagery more powerful or compelling than in the area of television news. Along with the spoken word, the visual image captures and documents the most important aspects of reality which both inform and entertain the mass audience. For those who study the form and content of news, the visual narrative structure becomes the focus of interest. Here it is that the artifacts of human behavior manifest themselves, offering critical bits of reality that help the audience piece together the stuff of everyday life.

The study of southern culture through the lens of the television news camera is what this paper is about. While a great deal of research has been conducted in visual anthropology, little if any work has focused on accessing television news archives. Perhaps this is because a large portion of film archives is so poorly maintained that it is unaccessible for research (Dearstyne 1987). The recent expansion of computer usage by some film archivists, however, raises hope of using information technology to "promote traditional archival goals" (Smither 1987: 327).

This discussion introduces the reader to the WSB Atlanta Television News Archive. The archive is a computer-indexed collection of newsreel footage dating back to the early 1950s. It is a rich historical resource documenting the images, sights, and sounds of the filmic South.

NEWS FOOTAGE AS ARTIFACTS

The archive consists of 675,000 video clips originally shot for inclusion in the nightly news programs of WSB Television. The collection is maintained at the University of Georgia in Athens and forms a magnificent resource well suited for research by sociologists, anthropologists, communication researchers, and historians.

During 1984, 1985, and 1986 the Instructional Resources Center on the University of Georgia campus received a complete news film collection of the past thirty years of broadcast news operations from WSB-TV. What the university acquired were the artifacts of news covering a period from about 1950 through 1975. Historic records indicate that most of the newsreel footage aired during this period was simply thrown into boxes, most of it on wound "cores." It was never intended for further use.

In the early 1950s, television programming developed and expanded in an effort to serve some of the 34 percent of national households equipped with television sets. The structure of news programming was radically different than it is today. The typical television broadcast was only fifteen minutes long. The news anchor read the day's events straight into the camera, backed up by whatever footage could be gathered (Diamond, 1975).[1] WSB routinely borrowed still photographs from the *Atlanta Constitution*, a newspaper owned by the Cox corporation, the parent company of WSB-TV. These static visuals were used to enhance WSB news programming. The visual footage presented on air was shot by a cameraperson using a Bell and Howell model 70DR film camera. This remained relatively unchanged until the early 1960s, when videotape was introduced. Even then, Auricon and Arriflex film cameras were used as auxiliaries to the new technology.

During the thirty-year period in which WSB continued to shoot and save its news film, other stations in the Atlanta market destroyed on-air news footage to save valuable storage space. In fact, this method of "cleaning house" was not limited just to local station practice. The NBC network in New York, needing more room in its Brooklyn warehouse, gave the order to gather up all film stock, put it on a barge, and dump it in the Atlantic Ocean. As a result of this limited vision for a future historical-cultural record, little precious footage from the earliest days of television (including kinescopes) is available today.

In concert with their vision of an audiovisual archive to preserve a record of the events that were shaping the South and the nation at the time, WSB management hired a team of professional archivists to begin logging and documentation of every piece of film before delivery to the University of Georgia. This action was to prove significant. WSB not only maintained a recorded history, it also made a record of everything contained on each reel of film. This action, so at odds with the practice of other stations, added to the richness and significance of the WSB archive collection, and distinguishes it from all other film collections of its type.

FORM AND CONTENT

Fletcher and Keenan (1983:6) characterize this WSB material as the output of a well-managed and prosperous station located in a state capital and regional banking and trading center: "Important stories collected during the 1960's, the period from which most of the black-and-white local footage dates, include the Civil Rights movement, school integration, Southern politics during a period of extraordinary social change. . . . The outtakes of these stories are at least as valuable as the stories themselves."

The content of the archive can be broken down into numerous categories. The collection contains mostly hard news stories along with a few documentaries. General subject areas include (1) a detailed history of the civil rights movement, (2) the economic and political dealings of the old and new South, (3) a representative sampling of the sociology of southern culture, and (4) various public and social rituals. The collection contains news stories that are (1) produced by sources external to the WSB operation, (2) black-and-white footage prepared by the station, (3) color film produced by WSB, (4) black-and-white film outtakes of local stories affecting Atlanta and the surrounding community, and (5) color film outtakes of both local and national stories.

Fletcher and Keenan (1983), who describe in detail each of these content categories, reviewed a sample of 674 news stories. More than thirty-two thousand feet of film totaling fifteen hours were analyzed for content. Local stories and outtakes shot in color accounted for 44 percent of the total film analyzed, mostly from 1969 to 1975; local stories and outtakes shot mostly from 1960 to 1975 in black and white accounted for 42 percent of the total film shot mostly from 1960 to 1975; finally, 14 percent of the total film shot in black and white and dealing with national stories came from sources outside WSB. Film in this last category was shot mainly from 1950 to 1966.

Physically the collection includes 2,527 reels of archival history. Each

Figure 1. Topical Index

Accidents, Disasters, Tragedies	Foreign countries, International relations
Animals	
Art, Music, Drama, Literature	Geography and geology
Astronomy, Atmosphere, Space, Weather	Holidays and special occasions
	Housing and furnishings
Blacks, Poverty, Civil rights movement	Labor activities, Issues, Unions
	Local politics and government
Business corporations	Medicine, Health, Human body
Business, Economics, Finance	Military
Clothing, Cosmetics, Jewelry	National politics and government
Communications	Organizations and clubs
Crime, Legal system	Physical science, Technology
Domestic relations, Family life	Plants
Education and schools	Protest groups, Causes, Minorities other than blacks
Entertainment, Amusements, Recreation, Sports	Religion
Food and beverages	State politics and government
	Transportation

reel contains twenty-three hundred feet of footage. A total of almost seventy thousand news stories are available for research purposes. Running time of each reel is approximately one hour. The total film length of the collection stands at about 4.7 million feet. All have been transferred to videotape to facilitate technological access.

What makes the WSB collection unique is the fact that it is fully indexed, modeling itself after the *New York Times* descriptor list. Thus researchers are given a wide range of topical areas to choose from. For instance, a scholar interested in exploring the sociology of domestic life might first turn to the topical index to see whether the subject is indexed (Fig. 1). The categories "domestic relations" and "family life" are listed, indicating that a more definitive subject area can be explored. Under the heading "Domestic relations, Family life," the researcher could then look for further descriptors that might help narrow the area of research concentration (see Fig. 2). Sociologists might be particularly interested in descriptors such as "battered spouses" and

Figure 2. Subindex for Domestic Relations, Family Life

Adoptions	Friends of Children
Alimony	Gifts
Baths and bathing	Home economics
Battered spouses	Housewives
Budgets and budgeting	Housework
Children and youth	Kissing
Community centers	Manners and customs
Community relations	Marriages
Consumer protection	Men
Consumers and consumption	Missing children
Consumers Union of U.S., Inc.	Missing persons
Cost of Living Council	Orphans and orphanages
Dating	Parents Anonymous
Day care centers for children	Pensions and retirement
Domestic relations	Recluses
Domestic service	Rehabilitation
Families and family life	Sex
Family and children services	Women
Foster care	

"missing children." Anthropologists might find fertile research areas associated with "manners and customs."

The proper names, dates, and places, once identified, can be easily coded for computer compilation and cross referencing. While the index is the most practical means of approaching a subject search there is no policy that would prohibit a scholar from suggesting additional descriptions that might serve to reveal highly specialized information. These could be used to research the descriptor line.

ACCESS TO THE COLLECTION

Typically the process of access is achieved through the following steps: a detailed letter of inquiry is sent to the director of the archive outlining the proposed research project.[2] The director's office reviews each application on a case-by-case basis, determining such things as feasibility of the search and compatibility with researcher needs. While one letter requesting access is all that is usually needed, more complex requests may require further explanation indicating subject matter and time frame. If it is deemed that the archive can be of direct benefit to the specific needs of a researcher, an initial computer run is conducted to sweep through the collection holdings.

An assistant is given key descriptor words matching the information provided by the scholar. These are provided by users who may request a search be conducted using their own key word list or one in which the WSB index has been accessed. Once entered into the computer, descriptors are cross tabulated, resulting in a record and summary of archival holdings matching the user requests. This output provides the researcher with a list of the total number of film holdings that fall under a requested topic area along with a summary statement typically indicating who or what might be on the tape (principals as well as other general descriptive information) and where the action occurred (locations).

At the scholar's request, a second computer run is carried out to get at the actual records. These include in detail (1) the record identification number, (2) the date the original film was shot, (3) the film reel number in which the artifact is stored, (4) the length of each version, (5) the location of each version within the master reel, (6) identification, if applicable, of the footage as being the "B" roll (more commonly referred to as the outtake footage), (7) accompanying script availability, and (8) a brief summary of what actually exists on the accessed film. (See Fig. 3.) Film footage is then pulled and reviewed either on site or elsewhere through special arrangement with the archive's director.

IMPLICATIONS FOR RESEARCH

Moving images, especially those which reflect past history, "satisfy a profound yearning for knowledge about ourselves and our roots" (Kuiper 1988: 49). As such, the WSB collection can be accessed and used to fulfill a number of scholarly endeavors. Among the possibilities are studies concerned with the analysis of visual forms. Historians may also find a rich array of materials that serve to elaborate upon a cultural and historical framework of the new and old South. Sociologists

Figure 3. Sample Summary Sheet

Record #: 42832   Date: 08/05/60   Film reel #: 0952

	Length	Time into reel	"B" roll	Script
Version 1	2:05	34:42		

Summary: Racists assemble in costumes; Ku Klux Klan funeral

Persons in story: A (audio bite)   N (no audio bite)

P1 Edwards, Eldon   N P2
P3   P4
P5   P6

Descriptors: P (person)   T (topical)   G (geographic loc)

D1 Ku Klux Klan   T D2 Funerals
D3 Blacks   T D4
D5   D6

Reporter: C/S   C/NS   BW/S   BW/NS
                                                          X

and anthropologists can look to the archive as a means of investigating the socio-cultural and historical record from different points and times. The collection is a rich database useful in the investigation of day-to-day life experiences that occur during and around significant events. The visual records of the collection can also be used as a way of looking more deeply into how social organization was achieved and maintained throughout the change and turmoil of the civil rights movement. Oral histories and performances of key figures of the day can be readily reviewed using the collection's computerized index.

Finally, film historians and social commentators might consider accessing the collection for two of its many unique treasures. The collection contains over two thousand hand-drawn "cartoons" originally aired by WSB as part of its nightly newscasts. The camera operator would scan the cartoon, allowing the home viewer to "text read" the slowly unfolding story. The object of this was to allow the camera to document the action for the viewer in a somewhat fluid manner, leaving the "punch" line till the end. Cartoons covering such topics as the legalization of marijuana, gun control, and the Ku Klux Klan are accompanied by graphic images and phraseology of the day. All these and more can be found residing in this resource.

Another area of particular interest, especially to the author, is a collection of hard-to-find cinema vérité news pieces in which we see only natural sound and visual actions. As the camera rolls uninterrupted (some pieces may go as long as eight minutes) the viewer is allowed to form impressions and generate meanings toward an interpretation of the behavior manifesting itself on the screen. Thanks to the filmmaker's ability to simply let the camera roll and record, the unedited film is a record of naturally occurring interaction.

In sum, the textual body of visual imagery found in the WSB collection is an important source of information for studying social organization and social life in the framework of a historic past. Like other film and video archives, WSB's problems with understaffing have limited development of the full range of services the archive can provide; however, plans are under way to increase staff positions and to further improve the automation of the data base. This continued commitment will aid in the future mining of the collection.

NOTES

The author wishes to thank John R. Stephens, Jr., director of the Instructional Resources Center at the University of Georgia, for his time and aid in preparing this document. Also thanks to Dr. James Fletcher, Department of Telecommunications, for reading this manuscript and making valuable comments along the way.

1. Diamond (1975) refers to the task of correspondents simply reading the news to the camera as "fringe news."
2. All correspondence can be addressed to: Director, Instructional Resources Center, University of Georgia, Athens, Ga. 30602.

REFERENCES

DEARSTYNE, BRUCE, 1987. What Is the Use of Archives? A Challenge for the Profession. *American Archivist* 50:76–87.
DIAMOND, EDWIN, 1975. *The Tin Kazoo* (Cambridge: MIT Press).
FLETCHER, JAMES, and KEVIN KEENAN, 1983. A Description and Appraisal of the WSB Television News-Film Library. Unpublished article.
KUIPER, JOHN, 1988. The Decade of Access? Moving Image Archives in the USA, a Retrospective Look and a Status Report. *Journal of Film and Video* 40:49–54.
SMITHER, ROGER, 1987. Formats and Standards: A Film Archive Perspective on Exchanging Computerized Data. *American Archivist* 50:324–37.

Was It Not Real? Democratizing Myth Through Ken Burns's *The Civil War*

James Peacock and Virginia Moore

> "The thing [the Civil War] was too big and too bloody, too full of suffering and hatred, and too closely knit into the fabric of our meaning as a people, to be held off and looked at—until now."
> —*Walker Percy,* 1991

The American Revolution inspired new nations, and perhaps the world wars saved the world for democracy, but the American Civil War best caught literary and film imagination. *Gone with the Wind* has sold more copies than any other book published in America, has been translated into twenty-eight languages, and continues to enjoy great success as a film. The Civil War remains seminal, for southerners and, to a degree, for the North and the world, as a frame to image the South. For the South, the Civil War is more than images. It is a myth, a cosmic frame, an epochal epic, a reservoir of tortured emotion: sadness, pride, regret, and resentment combined with inspiration and courage. We argue that Ken Burns stirs these emotions as he recounts the epic, but also "democratizes" this myth. He does this by welding myth to image.

As imaged, the South of the Civil War, especially for southerners, is mythological: sanctified, elevated, monumentalized, larger than life. True, the Civil War is imaged, especially by southerners, visually and to some extent musically—Dixie, the Stars and Bars, the Confederate soldier statue in the square, the antebellum mansions (fake or authentic), the portraits of Robert E. Lee. But like any myth, the meanings are not particularized through documentation so much as they are generalized through categories. The dichotomies (North and South, Yankee and Rebel, for instance) still carry a powerful emotional load. We shall suggest and describe some of the ways Ken Burns's film particularizes the myth by diffusing (hence de-fusing) the dichotomies. Such diffusing/defusing democratizes the myth by spreading its availability to the modern audience and by providing a variety of images that present/represent a wider range of voices from the war itself.

Burns meticulously and voluminously compiles period black-and-white photographs accompanied by poignant quotes from diaries, letters, and public documents of the time. These are juxtaposed against later film footage of reunions and comments from modern Civil War scholars, and interspersed with period music, color paintings, and modern sunrises on former battlefields. The sheer variety of the images renders the myth more democratic, less awesomely dichotomous.

We have no special cinemagraphic qualifications to comment on this masterpiece, but we approach it as anthropologists of the South. Much of our task will be simply to summarize the narrative and the images to help jog memories toward some kind of interpretation.

Does any single theme pervade the whole? Certainly, the theme of suffering is pervasive. Benedict Anderson, in *Imagined Communities* (1983), poses the great paradox of nationalism by suggesting that although a nation is an imagined community (and most members of a national community never know the other members and the community is limited because no nation claims to be the world) nationalism has produced more sacrifice and more killing than most forms of allegiance. Anderson attempts to explain this phenomenon and so does Burns, albeit the latter in a less theoretical way. The South and the Civil War are examples of extraordinary sacrifice and suffering for two different kinds of nationalist cause. The Federal forces fought to sustain a larger national unity and the Confederate forces attempted to create a new, smaller nation by secession from the prior Union.

Charles Joyner, in another television series called *Legacy of Conflict*, also deals with the Civil War, set in a South Carolina context. There he refers to tragedy, in the Greek sense, as dominating the Civil War for the South. Joyner implies tragedy not only in that an event is sad, for certainly the Civil War stands as a terribly sad event, but tragedy in the classical meaning where there is a predestination to events. Once events begin they cannot be stopped; it is as if they are foreordained. Burns's depiction of the Civil War frequently reflects this model.

Burns's *The Civil War* can be compared with *The Mahabharata*, a film that appeared on television around the same time as *The Civil War*. The "Mahabharata" is the great Hindu epic of the first millenium B.C., interpreted for stage by Peter Brook. It, too, features a sense of the inevitable, but in this film time is reversible—people can die but they can also be reborn; events happen but they can be undone. Time in *The Civil War* is irreversible and once something is done it cannot be undone. Events move along and terrible things happen, even though actors on both sides seem to have the best of intentions and some, like Robert E. Lee, seem to have such noble characters. Yet Lee and others find themselves commanding the murder of more people than in any other American war. This inevitability of history, leading ineluctably toward terrible suffering, produces the mythic aspect. How can the organization of *The Civil War* be summed up? The film is basically chronological, although there are a variety of cross-cutting themes.

The most memorable images are black-and-white photographs of the period that Ken Burns artfully edited. Sometimes they are introduced by modern footage showing silhouettes of cannon and sunset or scenes of the old battlefields carefully framed to avoid anachronistic buildings or automobiles. The black-and-white photographs become the markers of history, captured then, and the colored scenes provide the modern juxtaposition of our present with reference to that past. Commentators like Shelby Foote, Barbara Field, Stuart Symington, and Ed Bears are the modern historical scholars who bridge the past and present, providing color (to use a television phrase) to the black-and-white of photographs and history books. The sounds of the film, from the haunting violin theme repeated throughout to the cannon fire to the old marching songs to the comic play that was the occasion for the fatal gunshot wound to Lincoln, provide a different, more sensory depth to the photographs. Burns enlivens the stills by panning across them with the camera. This gives yet a further feeling of motion to scenes that might otherwise seem frozen by space and time. By panning photographs, as an eye might gaze upon a scene, the audience is invited to focus on parts of the picture (those which Burns deems the most important): to catch the foot soldier's eyes and then draw away to catch another man's eyes; to view a dead body on the side of the gully and then, as the camera pulls back, to see that body as one of hundreds strewn across a field.

The text is composed partly of omniscient narration, which comes through the emotionally neutralized voice of David McCullough. McCullough speaks with a basically straight American accent, neither high British nor low anything, not the oracular voice of time but a straight, descriptive voice that meticulously pinpoints qualities and features of events and characters. When he says of Stonewall Jackson that "he's a cold, blue-eyed killer," our instinct is to believe that it's true. This kind of matter-of-fact commentator, even when expressing an opinion, serves Burns in the task of democratizing the myth. McCullough takes a middle American role: biased toward neither side but framing the tragedy with a voice of reality, the voice perhaps of the many who were caught within the irreversible chain of events. Also, unlike the modern commentators (who fulfill a separate function), McCullough is rarely seen but remains only a voice, continually updating us through the chronology. McCullough and Shelby Foote can be compared with Don Meredith and Frank Gifford from the old days of Monday Night Football. Gifford (McCullough) provided the straight, precise play-by-play descriptions and Meredith (Foote) served as the comic, human, southern commentator with the deceptively easy concrete anecdote.

Much of the narration is drawn from letters and diaries of the time. Mary Chesnut's diaries and soldiers' letters, the writings of generals and of Lincoln and Frederick Douglass, all provide further depth to the visualizations. Mary Chesnut, whose words are read by Julie Harris, provides a counterpoint to the many men, both modern and period; her descriptions are at once wonderfully perceptive and wry and poignant. Morgan Freeman, as Frederick Douglass, is the eloquent spokesman of African-Americans providing an urgent twist to the northern position. Attitudes in the north ranged from Douglass's philosophical and practical insistence on equality to those of the northern sympathizers of the Confederacy who even rioted to protest the war.

Each of the nine episodes is divided into parts that provide crosscutting themes in a chronological schemata. The war starts and ends on the land of Mr. McLean, in northern and then southern Virginia. Burns uses this to set his whole story in a kind of "folksy" frame. McLean says, "The war began in my front yard and ended in my front parlor." When Grant and Lee are looking for a place to sign the truce at Appomattox, who should they find but this same man who had moved to southern Virginia in an attempt to get away from the war. That McLean helps to frame the story not only adds an individual tone but deepens its epic and tragic impact by suggesting that a cycle that was completed in history actually accomplished nothing except to return to its starting place.

This early section is accompanied by music and images of soldiers passing fields of destruction, and it is followed by statistics—more than three million men involved, more than six hundred thousand died. Shiloh, in two days of battle, produced more deaths than all other American wars up to that time, they say. And behind the statistics are reflections about the meaning of it all. Shelby Foote notes that "we used to say the United States *are;* now we say the United States *is.*" Purists could argue that this may actually merely represent a shift from British English to American English because British English would make the plural if it's a unit; for example, the team "are." His point, however, is that before the war we were a nation defined by regional interests; after the war we were a unity. These kinds of commentaries explain the chronology, merging the war with its effects.

"All Night Forever" shifts to the world of slaves. It begins with the singing of "Jacob's Ladder," panning shots of blacks and quoting a slave saying, "No day is ever dawning for the slave," and a white saying he'd rather be dead than a slave. This roots the epic in an essentially oppressive condition. This image is carried on in the "Are We Free" episode with William Lloyd Garrison's rhetoric about abolition. Mary Chesnut is introduced, pondering the incompatibility of temper between the slave-owning South and the industrial North, saying, "We hate each other so." A string of New England writers (Emerson, Hawthorne, and Melville), followed by Frederick Douglass, comment on John Brown's raid and execution. The tone then changes to reflect secessionist rhetoric, and there is an allusion to "the better angels of our nature," which becomes a major theme later on in the series.

Only one date is provided as a specific time and given its own section heading: 4:30 A.M. April 12, 1861. Brigadier-General Pierre Beauregard opens fire on his old West Point commander, Major Robert Anderson, at Fort Sumter. Supposedly, the first shot was fired by a civilian, Edmund Ruffin, from Virginia.

The "homey" theme continues into the battle of Bull Run, when picnickers came out from Washington to watch the sport. The Rebel yell was invented—yelling like Furies—although no one now knows what it sounds like because during the postwar reunions, former Confederate soldiers said they could do it properly only if they meant it, and staging a fake battle for a reunion would mean the Rebel yell was fake too. Thomas "Stonewall" Jackson gets his nickname at Bull Run. George McClellan is introduced as a thirty-four-year-old general with "an indescribable air of success, young Napoleon." The rank and file are introduced as little more than cannon fodder and are characterized as honorable manhood, the ones who will sacrifice themselves. Sullivan Belue, a northern soldier, writes home to his wife: "I am willing to lay down my life . . . my love for you is deathless, yet my love of country comes over me like a strong wind and bears me irresistably with chains to the battlefield. . . . If the dead come back, I shall be with you." He dies shortly after writing the letter.

From here, the series focuses on "the bloody affair," providing statistics on the assembled masses of common soldiers. The soldiers were, on average, five feet and eight inches tall, 143 pounds. One in thirteen died from disease; one in sixty-five died in combat. On average, they were twenty-five years old.

Shiloh is given its own heading, honored as the great place of destruction. Later, Shiloh becomes the comparator for the ordinary soldier: "I was worse scared then I was at Shiloh." Following a section on the weapons of destruction, the economic reality is shown from the common soldier's point of view; Sam Watkins, an enlisted Confederate, notes: "Rich man's war, poor man's fight. From this time on a soldier was a machine, a conscript. All our pride and valor were gone. We were sick of war and cursed the Confederacy." Watkins doesn't actually leave the fight but remains and becomes the foot soldier's most eloquent spokesman.

Stonewall Jackson is reintroduced and his relentless mix of war spirit and religious zeal is quoted: "It's a man's entire duty to pray and fight." His portrait makes him out to be a hawk-eyed, sharp-featured man.

"The Higher Object" refers to the freeing of the slaves, taking the war from political unionism to a higher moral ground, and coincides with the return of Ulysses S. Grant to a state of grace within the U.S. Army. John Stuart Mill says that "the South was made into evil and the war into a fight of good versus evil at the point when the war was transformed by the Emancipation Proclamation to a war to free the slaves." However, the "higher object" is quickly followed by an episode titled "Simply Murder," which focuses on the human destruction—the effect of the "noble" goals.

The death of Stonewall Jackson, the result of an accidental shooting by his own men following the battle of Chancellorsville, comes on Sunday, May 13. As he died, Jackson said, "Let us cross over the river and rest under the shade of the trees." His death is followed by the immediate introduction of "A Dust-Covered Man," U. S. Grant, who had been accused of stupidity, sloth, and drunkenness—practically the opposite traits applied to Jackson. And yet, one knows that Grant will stand and rise almost from the point at which Stonewall fell.

Gettysburg is divided into its three days, dwelling on the turning point. Then comes William Faulkner, from *Intruder in the Dust*, speaking of the hope of every southern boy to go back before the war was lost, to go back before Gettysburg, and imagine "what if?" But from this point, the South is shown to be losing. The siege at Vicksburg, for instance, shows people living in hillside caves, but ever defiant.

Another shift comes in the episode "Bottom Rail on Top." A former slave, now a Union soldier, greets his former master on the road by saying, "Hello Massah, bottom rail on top this time," demonstrating a profound and poignant level of change in social relations.

From time to time the narration tries to set the war in terms of world events. In 1864, as the Union forces prepare to attack Atlanta, *War and Peace* is published, Nevada becomes a state, and "In God We Trust" first appears on U.S. coins. The episode "Grant" uses aphorism to portray the general as a no-nonsense person—he once said he could recognize two tunes: "One of them is 'Yankee Doodle' and the other one isn't." A section titled "Lee" follows, with another appearance by Mary Chesnut: "Can anybody say they know the general? I doubt it. . . ." Lee, called "the Marble Man," is taken through the three phases of his life with his portraits: first as a handsome young man, without mustache; then as a middle-aged captain with a black mustache; finally, as the sainted general with a white beard. Once known as "Granny Lee" because he was thought to be hesitant, Lee disproved his detractors with his battle record.

Side scenes break into the narration of battle, showing things the soldiers did in daily life, outside of "history." There was betting on anything and everything, from cockfighting to races between fleas and lice. And the industrial and entrepreneurial conditions create "The Age of Shoddy," where "you can sell almost anything to the government . . . if you've got the guts to ask."

As a symbolic statement from the North to the South, Arlington

National Cemetery is created in Lee's front yard so that no one would ever want to live there again. Yet in the end this "Most Hallowed Ground" also serves to unify the country.

Sherman's entry is featured in "War Is All Hell": "My aim was to whip the rebels . . . make them fear and dread us. . . . War is all Hell. The crueler it is the sooner it'll be over." Shelby Foote calls Sherman the first modern general because he took war to the civilian population. With "Sherman's March" comes a plethora of comments, primarily from women. In spite of a policy of no plundering, Union soldiers could "kill, gut, and scrape a pig without breaking rank." Mary Chesnut notes that "they say no living thing is found in Sherman's track, only chimneys, like telegraph poles to carry the news of his attack backwards." Women, through their diaries, speak of the destruction and desperate times. Mary Chesnut despairs: "Darkest of all Decembers ever my life has known. Sitting here by the embers; stunned, helpless, alone." A Charleston woman says, "The wind moans among the bleak chimneys and whistles through the gaping windows. The market is a ruined shell, its spire fallen in. The old bell of secession that had rung out every state . . . lying half-buried in the Earth."

In "Died of a Theory," the noble principles of the Confederate myth are pitted against wasting reality. Jefferson Davis says, "If it [the Confederacy] falls, it should be written on its tombstone, died of a theory." Robert E. Lee went to the Confederate congress and noted that "they seem able to do nothing but eat peanuts and chew tobacco, while my army is starving."

In Washington in 1865, Abraham Lincoln writes, "I'm a tired man. Sometimes I think I'm the tiredest man on Earth." And yet the war is moving to conclusion. Stuart Symington movingly narrates the surrender at Appomattox. Then Burns steps out of the chronological story, commenting on the media during the war. Of note is that of the millions of photographs made during the war most were unwanted after the war and were thrown away. In some instances the glass was used as tile for greenhouses.

"The Better Angels of Our Nature" shifts us back into the story in 1865. The scene opens with "Yankee Doodle" played by a brass band. Lee has surrendered and people hope for the best. Mary Chesnut describes the psychological desolation in the South, saying, "We are scattered, stunned, the remnant of life within us is filled with brotherly hate. Whose fault? Everybody blamed by somebody else, only the dead heroes left stiff and stark escape." Edmund Ruffin, the man who fired the first shot at Fort Sumter, drapes a flag over himself and commits suicide. This is followed in the episode by the assassination of Lincoln and the subsequent tracking down and killing of Booth. Upon his death, Booth throws up his hand and shouts, "Useless, useless."

In "The Picklocks of Biographers," statistics are repeated: 3.5 million going to war, 620,000 dying, and so forth. Various voices give a further sense of the depth of feelings about the war. Sam Watkins notes, "In America there is no north, no south, no east, no west . . . the compass just points up and down and we can laugh now at the absurd notion" that there could be two different countries. Mary Chesnut bemoans "all that is past and gone." L. Stillwell, from Illinois, notes that the morning after getting home he "proceeded to wage war on the corn." This is followed by a recapitulation of what happened to the various major figures of the war. McClellan went abroad for three years so nobody would tell him the bad news of himself, then he returned to be elected governor of New Jersey; Beauregard started running a railroad and then a lottery in Louisiana; Nathan Bedford Forrest became Wizard of the Ku Klux Klan but quit when it became too violent even for his tastes. Lee, left jobless, was offered fifty thousand dollars for the use of his name, but he refused the money, saying he could not accept pay unless for services rendered. Grant, who later became president of the United States, gave his name to a brokerage, which bankrupted him with its criminal activities. Late in life, stricken with cancer, Grant heroically wrote his memoirs to provide some money for his family after his death.

The final section is titled "Was It Not Real?" and ends with Sam Watkins's meditation that someday death might be abolished, that the soldiers would fight but at the end the slain and wounded would get up and people from both sides would meet under the two flags to laugh and drink and ask, "Did it not seem real? Was it not as in the old days?" Again, Burns has returned us to a mythic level, although this time perhaps more in line with the Norse Valhalla or the Hindu Nirvana (very much like the end of *The Mahabharata* as depicted by Brooks). The self-questioning of reality, however, also suggests a dream-like dimension of the war. Watkins is not denying the war, the epic tragedy of both errors and successes; instead, perhaps, he struggles to resolve his (and the Union's) survival with the seen and known destruction of lives, property, and a way of life as the consequences of an irreversible chain of events.

Sam Watkins (C.S.A.) and Washington Roebling (U.S.A.) are the foot soldier's most poignant choral spokesmen. Watkins questions reality (the destruction as a vagary of his own imagination) yet holds onto hopes (that the dead and wounded will drink and laugh again with the living) that are juxtaposed against his hard and realistic cynicism (rich man's war, poor man's fight). Thus, *The Civil War*, with photos, music, quotes, and narration, mirrors this panoply of emotions.

What is the democratization of the myth, and how has Burns accomplished this? How has Burns achieved the visualization of the South? One aspect of democratizing a myth is to view a myth in its classic sense and compare it with its revised sense. In classical Greek myths, the actors were elites (or ordinary people raised to elite status in Ovid's Roman myths). The South's mythic "Lost Cause" centers on elite figures like Jefferson Davis, Stonewall Jackson, and Robert E. Lee and their noble ideals and principles. The dichotomies divide characters of North and South as good and bad, depending on how they foster or hinder the mythic elements. In democratizing the myth, Burns has not only shown the dichotomies to be false on military, political, and geographic lines (thus: desertions and spies), but he has also introduced varied visual and narrative images that demonstrate a depth and breadth to the actors' lives. Some of this is achieved in the endless photos of ordinary soldiers, normally the faceless chorus, whose eyes pierce beyond the television and seem to beg for recognition of their soul.

How does Burns translate mythological resonances into documentary images? Our contention is that he democratizes the myth simply by showing: by the black and white photographs and diary and letter narrations. The myth is sustained by terse, sometimes silent, commentary and implications: the veteran Union soldiers before the battle of Cold Harbor pinning name tags to their backs so that they could be identified among the dead the next day; the camera pans across an old black-and-white photograph of soldiers leaning against a roughhewn fence and an anonymous voice says, "This was no war. This was murder." The idealistic myth of great generals and noble principles is shifted to the foot soldiers' acceptance of fate, even death, as murder. In a social sense, *The Civil War* democratizes by giving solo, particular voice to those who are otherwise nameless and faceless. Watkins and Roebling become the primary spokesmen, although other chorus members are also given voice, sometimes with pictures and names, at other times as anonymous commentators.

The mythological dichotomies are particularized and expanded into complex reality. Boundaries, perceived as black and white in the myth, become blurred as documentary scenes juxtapose overlapping themes and conflicting ideals within geographic zones and even individuals. Split attitudes within families (such as the family members who meet on a Yankee ship during battle), riots in New York City, Union sympathizers in the South and Confederate sympathizers in the North, and spies and deserters all serve to break down the mythic dichotomies. The dichotomies of the myth, and their subsequent blurring, also enhance each other.

The visualization of the South deepens by the corresponding vision of the North. The fiction of indelible differences is erased by the parallels and similarities. The "lost cause" myth is transformed into a more encompassing perspective beyond slavery, Unionism, and agricultural/industrial economics. The myth turns into farm boys who before the war had never ventured more than twenty miles from their homes and then through the war came to know much of the country's land. The myth becomes the women at home who received the soulful letters of soldiers facing death, and the women who worked in the hospitals trying to patch men back together. The "lost cause" confronts slavery's "all night forever." And as Shelby Foote notes, the ideals of the United States "are" changes to the United States "is," with a corresponding shift in attitude. Perhaps this is a grammatical shift, but the images Burns presents demonstrate a deeper mental shift for Americans, the democratization of prior myths.

Time and space are bridged through the juxtaposition of pictures of war and postwar, of war and peace, and of contrasting genres: battlefields and farms, portraits and diaries, reunions and commentaries, recent images and moving pictures placed with the photographs of the earlier epoch. This message is, perhaps, that time heals wounds, but only through contextualization can the awful tragedies be resolved, by working them into ongoing social and cultural networks and processes. This includes the making of myths and documenting of history, as Burns achieves with *The Civil War*.

REFERENCES

ANDERSON, BENEDICT, 1983. *Imagined Communities: Reflections on the Origin and Spread of Nationalism* (London: Verso Press).
PERCY, WALKER, 1991. The American War. In *Signposts in a Strange Land*, Patrick Samway, ed. (New York: Farrar, Straus & Giroux), p. 72. Originally published 1957 in *Commonweal* 65: 655–57.

PART 3
Statements from the People

Twixt the Holler and the Mall: Appalshop Films and the Politics of Image in an Eastern Kentucky Classroom

Robert Gipe and Ann Messer

PROLOGUE: IN WHICH EVERYBODY IS
SOMEBODY'S HILLBILLY

> *May 15, 1991: I think all Whitesburg Middle School cheerleaders are snobs. (From a cheerleader at Cowan)*
>
> *May 22, 1991: To the cheerleaders at Cowan from the cheerleaders at Whitesburg—stick it where the sun doesn't shine. And don't be mean to us just because we're the best. We can't help it, you know. (From a student at Whitesburg)*
>
> *May 22, 1991: To the Cowan cheerleaders who said all of Whitesburg's cheerleaders are snobs—you got a lot of room to talk.*
>
> *June 12, 1991: To Cowan's cheerleaders from Whitesburg: we might not have won this year, but at least we don't do the same cheer every year.*

Letcher County is in southeastern Kentucky. Its leading industry is coal. Its terrain is mountainous, and its population is around twenty-seven thousand people. The above excerpts from "Speak Your Piece," the phone-in public opinion forum in *The Mountain Eagle*, a Letcher County newspaper, come from Cowan, in the south-central part of the county, and Whitesburg, the county seat.[1] In Letcher County, Whitesburg—population twelve hundred—is "town." The courthouse is there. The Wal-Mart is there. "Country" people live out from town, in places like Campbells Branch and Kingdom Come Creek, Carcassonne and Cowan. Kingsport, Tennessee, is an hour and a half south of the Letcher County line, down U.S. Route 23. Kingsport is a factory town of thirty-five thousand people, with large Eastman Kodak and Mead Paper installations. To most students in Kingsport, people in Letcher County are *all* country people, "hillbillies," who descend on Kingsport's malls around Christmastime because there are no malls in southeastern Kentucky.

Engineers and marketing executives from Chicago sometimes come to Kingsport to work at Eastman Kodak. Their children generally consider the kids from Kingsport hicks, with little to distinguish them from kids in Letcher County. Many of these kids from Chicago will have family, grandmothers even, from eastern Kentucky. They love their grandmothers dearly but would still be mortified if anybody at school found out that Mamaw coated their chest with cooked onions any time they had a cold.

To many, this circle of namecalling and defining oneself against one's image of someone else will seem ironic—but when one is in the ninth grade, developing a sense of irony is not nearly as important as eating lunch at the right table.

THE APPALSHOP SCHOOL INITIATIVE

I-75 is the closest interstate highway to Letcher County. It runs along the western edge of the eastern Kentucky coalfields. I-75 runs right through Laurel County, some seventy miles west of Whitesburg. For a student at South Laurel County Junior High School, less than an hour to the north on I-75 waits Lexington, a city of 160,000, in the heart of the Bluegrass section of the state, where malls and shopping plazas unfold in dazzling succession, where luxury cars spirit smartly dressed urban professionals between the racetrack and lower arena seats at University of Kentucky basketball games. Televised music videos prophesy a promised land of expensive basketball shoes, rock concerts, and fifty-dollar asymmetrical haircuts. For many a mountain youth, including those at South Laurel Junior High School, Lexington is a consumer Canaan.

Ann Messer teaches ninth-grade English at South Laurel Junior High School. She is also a member of the Eastern Kentucky Teachers Network. The Teachers Network is one of ten in the Foxfire Teacher Outreach project. Foxfire is a teaching approach developed by high school English teacher Eliot Wigginton and his students in north Georgia. Foxfire teaching stresses hands-on work for students, student involvement in the design of their own learning process, and student work that involves the larger community as both subject and audience.

Messer is also one of the teacher-researchers in the Appalshop School Initiative. Appalshop is a media arts center with headquarters in Whitesburg. It began in 1969 as an experiment in hands-on learning initiated by the federal government's Office of Economic Opportunity and the American Film Institute. The Appalachian Community Film Workshop, as Appalshop was originally known, was intended to teach young people how to make films and television programs so that they could leave the mountains and find jobs in the communications industry. When the student filmmakers, many fresh out of high school, began documenting life in and around Whitesburg as a way of learning the tools of the media artist's trade, they began to look at the people of the area differently. As they did, the mission of the Appalachian Community Film Workshop began to change.

Herb E. Smith is a graduate of Whitesburg High School and one of the original film workshop trainees. He continues to make films at Appalshop and explained some of the forces that led the original Appalshop filmmakers to try to make a go of it in Whitesburg:

> As we started going out and shooting these films, or as we started going out and talking to people in a way that we hadn't done growing up here . . . as a reporter, people have access, you can ask me all kinds of questions that if you weren't interviewing me, you wouldn't feel comfortable in asking. . . . The same kind of things happened with our film making, at least did with us that summer as we started going out and interviewing and talking about life in this part of the country. We began to understand this place in a way that we hadn't until that point. There was a strong sense in a lot of us that it was important that we stayed here and tried to create jobs for ourselves outside the coal industry. . . . Part of it came from that experience of knowing who we were and where we were from in a way that was very positive. (Smith and Lewis 1984)

Appalshop began at a time when the coal counties of southern Appalachia had been the subject of considerable scrutiny in the national media. Coal employment had reached a low ebb in the late 1950s and 1960s, and Appalachia had been a prime front in the federal government's War on Poverty. As attention focused on the region from outside, and national magazines and television networks distributed images of poverty in the mountains to the world, the self-perception of people living in the mountains was affected. Jeff Kiser, a Letcher County native and former actor in Appalshop's Roadside Theater, explained the effect these images had on his growing up in the Appalshop film *Strangers and Kin*:

> I was almost too young to really have a good strong opinion one way or the other about it, but I can remember seeing people that I knew in their little tarpaper shacks and things laid out in them big color spreads in *Life* magazine and things, you know. And I used to think, God, what if that was us, you know, and I'd have to go to school and play with them boys during recess and things. I never would mention it to them, and they never would mention it, but it was there, everybody knowed it, you know, and I can remember many a time, coming home from school and walking into the yard and looking real close at what we had thinking how lucky we was, you know. And I used to think if it had been my family they had put in the magazine I probably never would have come back out of the holler. I would have quit school, probably. I would have been real upset. It would have definitely changed my way of thinking.

Those representations shaped the way Appalshop produces media. Part of Appalshop's mission has been to give access to the microphone and the camera to the people of the mountains who have been discussed and explained by outsiders so they can give their own account of their history and circumstances. Over the years, Appalshop has added a storytelling theater company (Roadside Theater), a documentary recording label (June Appal Recordings), and a community radio station (WMMT-FM) to its film- and videomaking operation. In the process, it has grown into one of the leading sources of audiovisual documentation of life in the southern Appalachians produced from within the mountains. It has produced more than seventy film and video documentaries and distributes its work through television broadcasts and cablecasts, screenings internationally, and sales to schools, colleges, libraries, and community groups.

The Appalshop School Initiative grew out of a need to serve one of the most grossly underserved and important audiences for Appalshop film and video: the public schools of eastern Kentucky and southwest Virginia. The project is an experiment in classroom research, where Appalshop grants taped copies of Appalshop films and videos to interested teachers and enters into research partnerships with those teachers to explore how the tapes can be integrated into the curriculum. The project goals for the School Initiative are different for different teachers. Some of the primary goals are

1. To help students define their individual relation to Appalachia by making the region part of their curriculum;
2. To develop media literacy so that students will be more active media consumers, particularly in identifying sources of media and the different biases of the different sources;
3. To develop critical thinking so that students will see themselves as more conscious, active participants in the creation of their own lives, media, education, career, family, political views, and so forth.

The project, designed in concert with the Eastern Kentucky Teachers Network, began in 1989. More than one thousand tapes have gone out to interested public school teachers in grades K–12. These teachers are providing Appalshop with a data base on how they are using the tapes. Fifteen of the teachers have become research partners and are documenting not just what they are doing with the tapes but also the overall changes in their teaching wrought by exposure to Foxfire, Appalshop, and the act of doing research. Ann Messer is one of these research partners.

So far we are learning that student reactions to Appalshop film and video and to images of Appalachia generally are strong but widely varied. Often, as in the case of South Laurel Junior High School, the reaction is outspokenly negative, at least in the beginning. To understand the reason students react the way they do, School Initiative project participants are learning how important it is to come to terms with the social geography—as well as the socioeconomics—of eastern Kentucky and the surrounding area. We are learning to make distinctions not just between city kids and country kids but among kids who live near an interstate highway, kids who do not live near interstates, kids who have moved from the mountains to other places and returned, country kids who live in the small towns and county seats, country kids who live back in the "hollers," kids who live in the mountains but not in the coal counties, and kids who consider themselves southern but not Appalachian.

Even when the lay of the land has been established, the reactions to images of Appalachia can still surprise. What follows is an account of Ann Messer's experimentation with Appalshop videos in school year 1990–91. In the early spring of the year, she said, "The hardest thing is getting kids to reason things out. That's probably because they spend so much time sitting passively in front of the TV." Over the course of the year, Ann and Appalshop worked together to get her students to approach media less passively and more critically, and as we did, we met a few surprises that had us doing some critical thinking of our own.

WATCHING FILMS

ANN MESSER: In the fall of 1990, my students and I embarked on the Appalshop School Initiative. We were to make a study of our responses to media and how Appalachian people were being represented through media, using Appalshop videos as a resource. As a Foxfire teacher, I was also interested in using the videos as a springboard to hands-on activities.

My students were ninth graders in London, Kentucky, a town located in the foothills of the Appalachian mountains but also bordering on the Bluegrass region. Some of my students have deep roots in the rolling hills of Laurel County and have lived there all their lives. Others had roots in the coal counties to the east. For instance, both sets of one student's grandparents were from around Hazard, in the heart of the coalfields, and she visited there at least once a month. Others had the common eastern Kentucky experience of more than one move into and out of the mountains. One student had lived in Cincinnati, Miami, and Oregon. At least one student had spent his early adolescent years in Lexington. About half considered themselves country kids and the other half described themselves as city kids.

My idea was that we would watch the videos and do some sort of project in response to one or more of them. We started with a film about Minnie Black, a local craftsperson. Minnie is the subject of *Minnie Black's Gourd Band*, part of a 1988 Appalshop TV series called "Headwaters." The students loved Minnie right away, so we invited her to visit our classroom. She came, and we learned about gourds and practiced interview techniques.

Conveniently, it was time for a field trip that we had scheduled to visit

James Still. James Still is a poet, short story writer, and novelist living in Hindman. The class was reading his novel *River of Earth* (1940), about the early days of large-scale coal mining in eastern Kentucky. In preparation for the visit to Still's cabin on Troublesome Creek, we saw the video film *Man on Troublesome* (1988).[2] It was exciting to get acquainted via film with someone who wrote a book that we were reading and whom we were to meet.

Our trip to Hindman was great, so I thought we were ready to see some kids from what I considered "our" area. It seemed a perfect time to view *Portraits and Dreams* (1984), a video film about a photography project carried out by a group of elementary school students in Letcher County, Kentucky, and get started on a project that we could present to Appalshop at the end of the year. In *Portraits and Dreams*, elementary students from three country schools in Letcher County photographed their families, their dreams, their animals, and other aspects of their lives under the tutelage of professional photographer Wendy Ewald. The photographs were taken between 1976 and 1981, and in the video the students talk with Ewald and Appalshop film- and videomaker Andy Garrison about making the photographs and growing up in the mountains. I introduced the film, showing the students that we had a classroom Polaroid, and suggested that we might get interested in a similar project. Confidently, I started the video.

I must have been pretty engrossed in the tape, because I didn't notice the transformation that was taking place in my classroom while the lights were out. When the lights came up the students were angry at the images they had seen and the voices they had heard. " I saw a bunch of hicks living in dumps and making pictures of themselves" was typical of the responses the students wrote. After that, attitudes changed. I just couldn't find a film that impressed them.

Why had the students reacted so negatively to *Portraits and Dreams* when they hadn't to the videos of James Still and Minnie Black? Many voiced concern that someone from outside Kentucky would identify the kids in *Portraits and Dreams*—with their pronounced mountain accents, modest houses, and yards full of animals—with them. In addition, both Still and Black had reputations that preceded them into the classroom. Still was a published author, which gave him a certain credibility. Black, for her part, had been on "The Tonight Show" and "Late Night with David Letterman." Both had been confirmed, in their own ways, by the larger culture. The student-photographers in *Portraits and Dreams* had no such confirmation.

To try to understand what had happened with my students when they saw *Portraits and Dreams*, I went back to an introduction to the video written by Wendy Ewald and compared her students with mine. Ewald wrote, "The children were already keen observers. Their parents taught them respect for and fear of their surroundings. They watch the crops grow, the seasons change, the animals being born and slaughtered, and when the boys go hunting they sit quietly watching and listening for signs of nearby animals." This is not the world of my students, except maybe for a few of the boys that hunt. My students generally have mobility and money; they are watching television instead of their surroundings. And those who might fit this description in my class would never admit it in front of their peers.

Ewald continued, "Their photographs speak from within their lives and record moments that suggest rhythms of everyday life. The world they present is small and intimate, but their perception of it is detailed, accepting, and complex." At the time we watched this video, my students had not developed their critical thinking skills enough to perceive what the Letcher County students were trying to say with their photographs. My students just saw a lifestyle with which they refused to associate themselves.

At the end of the project Ewald said that "each student explained what he wanted to show in his pictures, while the others told him what they saw. In this way he was able to distinguish between his feelings for the person or event in the picture and the emotional impact of the photograph itself." My students were not able to make that distinction, so they reacted negatively to the film and to the boys and girls because they did not like the emotions the photographs made them feel. At this point, the class would not willingly watch "hillbilly" movies for fear they would be considered hillbillies themselves.

This revulsion put our study in limbo until Robert Gipe came to the classroom and talked with the kids about the videos and their reactions to them. The students seemed more free to talk with him than me, in part because, in his unlaced hightops, he was a not-very-intimidating representative of the producers of the videos. Gipe also talked about being from Kingsport, on the borders of Appalachia, and having a high school setting much like theirs. The class talked about where the images came from and about distinguishing the different reasons for images made by different people. While Gipe was there, the class rewatched *Portraits and Dreams* and started on *Strangers and Kin* (1984).

ROBERT GIPE: *Strangers and Kin* is the first film in a proposed six-part series of Appalshop films on the history of Appalachia. It is an examination of the history of images of Appalachians in the press, in film and on television, and in the minds of people both inside and outside the region. It includes Roadside Theater actors and actresses dramatizing readings of George Washington Harris's Sut Lovingood stories, late-nineteenth-century pulp fiction, and the words of historians, journalists, industrialists, and philanthropists who cast mountain people in a negative light to help them, make fun of them, or exploit them. The film also includes television and film representations of Appalachians, from *Deliverance* to Ma and Pa Kettle, from Lil' Abner to TVA propaganda films, from War on Poverty news reports of Walter Cronkite and Charles Kuralt ("Depressed Area, U.S.A." and "Christmas in Appalachia") to "The Beverly Hillbillies." These scenes are intercut with scenes of contemporary Appalachia (including some from Appalshop Films) and interviews with the Roadside actors who raise questions about definitions of "progress" and whether the "development" of "backward" Appalachians by outsiders and insiders has been to positive effect. It is one of Appalshop's most challenging and often misunderstood films, because in presenting the negative images generated by outsiders (and occasionally by insiders), it expects the viewer to recognize that these images are being presented as part of an examination of the sources of images and the ways images can be exploited by the image generator. The film raises questions about the wages of not having control of the production and distribution of one's own image.

Strangers and Kin is a discussion film, not one designed to propagate any point of view. But some audiences have reacted to the presentation of the negative image as one might at the opening of an old wound, and discussion of the context in which the images are presented has been short-circuited by the strong emotions the film evokes in some mountain audiences. The images the Letcher County children presented in *Portraits and Dreams* and that Ewald and videographer Andy Garrison re-presented in the video caused the same sort of strong reaction in many of Messer's students as did *Strangers and Kin*. That reaction made it difficult to generate discussion about any of the issues raised by the tapes.

ANN MESSER: As I watched Gipe view parts of *Strangers and Kin* with my students, I realized that they were quite capable of becoming involved with the technical side of the films if not the subject matter. As we talked in class the next day about the way *Strangers and Kin* was constructed, the idea of breaking down the films formally, rather than focusing on content, evolved.

We started our plan for a critique sheet by filling the chalkboard with what we thought were important technical elements of a film. One of the kids then grouped the elements by connecting related ones with big circles. These groups were organized into a formal outline for our first critique sheet. By the next day I typed up the sheet with the title "Critique Sheet—First Effort." We studied the sheet, then we used it as we viewed *Catfish: Man of the Woods* (1974), a film about a man who lives alone and earns a living by finding and selling herbs. To our surprise, everyone paid attention and responded to the video. Our next step was to look at what we had done and see what worked and what didn't work. A great deal of discussion went into making changes, thus evolving four editions of the critique sheet and a pattern of use, then evaluation, then change. By the end of the year, we had developed a critique sheet that gave the students a framework for analyzing the films and videos on the basis of, among other things, sound, color, photography, scenery, quality of interviews and editing, transitions, and eventually, content.

ROBERT GIPE: Up until the time the students began using the critique sheets, they were seeing media makers as some outside "they" who seemed to be, at least in the case of Appalachian images, up to no good and over whom they had no control. As they got deeper into criticism and analysis of the construction of the films, and more comfortable with the vocabulary of the filmmaker, the films seemed to be coming from a less distant place. The filmmaker became less "other." As the filmmaker became less other, and as the class began to spend more time watching the videos, they seemed to get some perspective on the content and could return to it gradually, more subtle in their perception of the relation between the subject and the maker of the films. Meaning became something they could question, something less inviolate. Meaning began to have a certain pliability.

ANN MESSER: As the class watched more videos using the critique sheets, they began to wonder whether people's words in the films were unsolicited or were prompted by unheard questions from the filmmaker that were edited out of the final film. They began to wonder why this or that seemed important to the editors to include. They wondered if a ginseng digger in *Catfish* just happened to show up or whether his visit had been choreographed.

ROBERT GIPE: Perhaps the more the class thought about how films were put together, the less they perceived the media maker as a trickster who was going to get anything over on them. They were teaching themselves the tricks. Whether the maker was from the region or not, they were making their relation to the Appalachian image-trafficker less adversarial by putting themselves on a more even footing. Also, by studying the formal aspects of the films, they were distracting themselves from the accents. But what they were thinking about led them back into an examination of why these tapes were there, and back into the content.

During this time, Roadside Theater did a storytelling residency with Messer's class. Part of their work involved the grounding of certain Appalachian folktales (the "Jack" tales) in the tradition of Western literature (for example, the story of "Johnny Sore-Navel" and his escape from the one-eyed giant's lair as a version of the tale from *The Odyssey*).

ANN MESSER: My students saw the Roadside people as professional actors, which made it easier for them to validate the things Roadside said. These performers were proud of their heritage and of the culture they were representing, thus giving the students "permission" to explore their own culture. At this point, I found it interesting that my students did not even notice that Roadside's Ron Short had the same accent that they had found so offensive in the children of *Portraits and Dreams*.

ROBERT GIPE: Later, when Messer's students were interviewed about their feelings on being considered country kids, many of their responses indicated that they were seeing that label as positive. The following are some of their responses:

> INGRID: You just get used to it [being called a hillbilly]. If you have a problem with where you live then you're not going to let it bother you, but if you're ashamed of it, it's going to bother you. I'm not ashamed of it.
>
> JEFF (on the overemphasis on the material things in the city): They'll be your friend as long as you drive a Mercedes. It's not like that back in the country.
>
> BRANDON (on Appalshop videos): They don't have people that say stuff they really don't mean. . . . They're telling the truth the way they really feel.

These students were among the most indignant at the images in *Portraits and Dreams* and *Strangers and Kin*. Messer felt that the two main influences that changed their attitudes about the depiction of rural people in the videos and their own perceptions of themselves as rural people were the critical distance they gained on the videos (and themselves) through formal analysis and Roadside's Appalachian consciousness-raising.

ANN MESSER: In discussions with the class and then separately in discussions with Gipe, I realized that viewing the films critically set the students free to respond more objectively to the content. They didn't have to be so personally involved or put down by the content of the films. One girl in the class, Amanda, explained the process:

> When we first started watching the films, I didn't like them. The first couple we watched—and *Portraits and Dreams* was, like, the second one we watched—it was like they were kind of making fun, but like Roadside came and explained some of it, and that was fun, and then we got to meet some of the people that the films were about. That sort of made them a little better, but they still weren't that interesting. Then we made our critique sheets and we removed ourselves from them and watched them that way and they got a lot better. . . . We stopped looking at them like they were just about us, making fun of us, and we were just critics, just watching the films.

I began to notice that the class was looking past the surface, the accents and the clothes and the houses, and were starting to identify with people they might not have earlier. I first noticed this after we viewed a film entitled *On Our Own Land* (1988), which dealt with the injustices wrought by the broad form deed in eastern Kentucky in which exploitation of subsurface mineral rights by mining companies destroyed much property. Some of the students became angry at the situation they saw portrayed; others expressed concern because their fathers had jobs related to the strip-mining industry.

In March, Robert Gipe and Suzi Wehling, a videomaker working at Appalshop at the time, taped interviews with the students for use in our presentation at the Key Symposium. The questions came from Gipe and Wehling and from lists the students developed. The questions centered on how the students thought other people perceived Appalachian young people and their own expression of their culture. The students gladly shared their perceptions with Gipe and Wehling, neither of whom is an eastern Kentucky native. They had, however, established a common ground with the students based on a genuine interest in what the students were doing. The result of the taping was a sharing by the students of visual and verbal images of themselves, in some ways like the interviews with the children in *Portraits and Dreams*.

Becoming subjects of a video gave the students new insight into the productions they had seen. They noticed that Wehling and Gipe had shot all day for a five-minute tape, which made them wonder how much shooting was left out of the other productions they had seen and led back into discussions about the editing of those productions.

At the end of the school year, the critique sheets still were not completed. Although the students were able to use what we had in order to look critically at classroom films and television programs they watched at home, they still realized that there was room to go further into what they were doing. I hope that an important end result of this classroom research is that my students developed an ability to look critically at any visual medium they encounter, whether it is an instructional video, a documentary film, a television program, or a movie. I hope this will help them make appropriate choices about what to watch and how to assimilate what they do watch.

But even as the year ended, I began to question how my students came to be so involved in the content of the films when they had had such an adverse reaction to them earlier. My first thought was, "Well, with *On Our Own Land*, I have finally found something they like." I don't think that was the case, though, because they continued to be able to discuss even films that they disagreed with or that they felt were not presented in the best possible way. It seems more likely that withdrawing personally from the films and becoming critics took away the threat that they felt in seeing themselves in the films. At first the students saw the filmmaker as being on one level and the subjects of the films, with whom the students themselves related, on an inferior level, because they perceived that somebody else had control of the image. Becoming critics empowered them and gave them a greater sense of control over what they did with the films. With that empowerment came the ability to risk looking at what was there.

I am still trying to put together all the things I learned through this year of research with my students. Four thoughts surface:

1. We are better able to examine ourselves than we are able to accept examination of ourselves by outsiders. If we do accept examination by outsiders, we can open ourselves to them more easily if we feel that those outsiders have established a common ground with us.
2. My students might never have been willing to examine themselves without being challenged by examination by outsiders. Confrontation with other people's perception of us is a necessary part of our own self-definition.
3. In order for us, or any group, to accept our culture, we must be given permission to take pride in it. How do we get permission? Is it possible that that permission can come by seeing acceptance through the eyes of others? From Roadside Theater and the Appalshop videos we learned that one can give oneself permission.
4. The fourth thought comes from considering the tape Wehling and Gipe made with my students. Isn't that tape similar in some ways to *Portraits and Dreams*? The difference is that with our tape, my students were the filmmakers, not simply the subjects of a film made by outsiders, as they saw *Portraits and Dreams* to be. By the end of the spring's exploration, they had developed the ability—possibly even the need—to examine their own views of themselves, without considering what outsiders would think of them. Their new position was a union of being filmmakers and subjects.

ROBERT GIPE: These thoughts of Messer's bring some questions and concerns of mine out. Did her class see Appalshop film- and video-makers as insiders or outsiders? Could they now watch *Portraits and Dreams*, realizing that there is a difference in the presentation of life in Letcher County when it is done by schoolchildren living in the county and when it is done by *Life* magazine? One reason for concern were these comments from Messer's students in interviews toward the end of the year:

> BRANDON: We're not getting a fair turn. When they go to get an interview of somebody from Kentucky, somehow or another they always end up way up here [points up and away] talking to people in someplace with population fifteen, and they get those people but they don't ever give us a chance, you know.
>
> TONYA: Instead of showing films about what's wrong with Kentucky, they need to start showing films about what's good about Kentucky, because to people in other states who haven't visited us here, they don't really know what we're like, so if they see a film that's about something really really bad, something that's going, like, wrong. . . . We need to show something that's good that's happening here instead of something that's bad.
>
> INGRID: They always depict us as being lower than, inferior to, everybody else. And we're not that.

It seems that these kids were still coming to terms with the fact that one could present Appalachia as a distinct region, as different from other parts of the country (including that abstract realm represented as America on commercial television) without presenting it as negative.

Some questions still need to be investigated: Are Messer's students learning to make distinctions as to the source and reason behind various representations of mountain people? For example, can they make distinctions between a Roadside actor's presentation of Sut Lovingood in *Strangers and Kin*, Harris's presentation of Sut, traditional storyteller Ray Hicks presenting himself, and Appalshop filmmakers presenting Ray in a film? Are they seeing the two reactions a mountain person can have to an image of mountain people generated by outsiders that the outsiders consider a negative image? That is, (1) the mountain person can replace the outsider image with a more "positive" image that shows mountain people adopting a values system like the one the outsider holds, or (2) the mountain person can present the image the outsider presents in such a way that the viewer recognizes the value in the image that the outsider devalues.

ANN MESSER: It took a longer time to get these kids to share themselves than maybe it would have with the kids in *Portraits and Dreams*. Maybe this is because the kids in *Portraits and Dreams*, as part of a close-knit, tradition-bound community, were more comfortable with who they were. Or maybe it was because they were younger than my students and less acutely concerned about what others would think about them. Also, kids today may be under more pressure to look, dress, and act a certain way because of the greater amount of television and advertising to which they are exposed compared to what the *Portraits and Dreams* kids were seeing between 1976 and 1981 in and around Cowan, Kingdom Come, and Campbells Branch.

ROBERT GIPE: Ann, what have you learned about working through students' negative reactions to images of mountain people? Could you get them past these negative reactions more quickly now and move on to hands-on media projects like you had originally intended when you showed *Portraits and Dreams*?

ANN MESSER: I'm not sure that the way we went about it was wrong. We had to dive in and look at the images and then gauge the reaction of the kids. It still seems like a natural course to take to understand something about the politics of images before you begin making them. The shock of seeing and reacting to *Portraits and Dreams* challenged them to think about themselves in ways that they would not have done otherwise. The kids have to be slapped in the face with those negative images. They have to think along with you. The confrontation with what they don't want to think about is important. This year it happened by coincidence. Next year we can plan the confrontation.

Also, one has to be realistic about what you set out to accomplish in fifteen weeks. They may not have done a hands-on project, but they did more critical thinking than they would have if they had done a hands-on project without all this probing. This year they didn't get to their own production, but I hope that if they do some kind of media project next year, it will have more depth.

No one is well served if we as educators diminish or explain away the complexity of programs like *Strangers and Kin* and *Portraits and Dreams*. Students need to confront the world in all its complexity and think through it, balancing emotional reactions with critical and analytic ones. Students need to be encouraged to become both thinkers and feelers. In the case of the ninth-grade English class at South Laurel Junior High School, developing a knowledge of the means of production of Appalshop film and video helped give them a way to balance their strong emotional reaction to the tapes.

The students in Ann Messer's ninth-grade English class are not now totally sophisticated media consumers. It would be idealistic to say that they will always be perceptive enough to automatically begin tracing media images back to their source and analyze the reason why those images are being fed to them, particularly images that play to their emotions. Nor have they answered (or in some cases asked) some important questions about the relation of their attitude toward "hillbillies" and the construction of their own values system. However, these students came into their ninth-grade English class expecting to be given stories to read, surface comprehension questions to answer, and grammar worksheets to fill out—and little else. Messer's ability to react to her students' responses to the Appalshop tapes allowed them to go further, to find out some things for themselves about *how* they learn and form opinions. Her patience and persistence are important. A functioning democracy needs all of us to be readers, in the broadest sense, who understand that the meaning of a given image is the creation of audience as well as producer and must be constantly negotiated between the two.

It is an ongoing struggle for all of us to consciously shape the way we perceive television and other texts so that our interpretation includes both emotional and intellectual response. Messer's students made a start. As educators, we can take heart from one student's response to this statement in *On Our Own Land*:

> If we don't get a law to stop it it's just gonna go on and on. You see that mountain over there? Well, one day there won't be a mountain there if we can't get this broadform deed amendment thing a-going. I just stand here and think, Lord, when will I see them over there with a bulldozer tearing that down. It hurts. Thinking you'll have to see every bit of this tore down around you.
>
> What's been done over there has been done just for a few dollars and the dollars are spent. Now what have they got? Nothing. But that unsightly scene. And their water all destroyed. I heard that woman say she was a fool for letting them do it. She said, "I ought to have been like you. I'm a fool

for what I've done." Well, I don't see dollar signs. I could use money, sure. But I'll get by. My land's still like it was. They tried to establish me a pauper in the courts. I guess maybe they think I'm a pauper. The lawyer asked me if I knew what the word pauper meant, of all things, in the court. You know that's almost degrading you. I said, "I will beat you and I don't have to have money." My husband when he was sick he asked us to not let them [stripmine our land]. And you know we're gonna respect that wish, ain't we? What kind of people would we be if we didn't? People will say to me, "Oh, why don't you just sell out to them, get on away, you know you can use the money, let them go in there." I said, "Ain't no way. As long as they is a Wooten lives of this family, they'll not strip it."

The speaker, Elizabeth Wooten, does not speak standard English. By her own admission, she is not wealthy, and she lives back in the mountains where the Laurel County students said they wish filmmakers would not go. *On Our Own Land* talks about problems in the mountains, but when interviewed about why she responded favorably to the tape, one of the students said:

"*On Our Own Land* was different from *Strangers and Kin*. It showed how people are walking all over us and we're trying to do something about it. But in *Strangers and Kin*, it was showing the way that everybody depicted us and we don't care about it. [pause] You know, I guess they're both the same. I guess they are. I guess I was just looking at it in a different light."

This student may not have thought much about *Strangers and Kin* since she made this connection. She may not see through the next media ruse that plays to her base emotions, be it Willie Horton–style political ads or Bud Dry commercials asking her, "Why Ask Why?" But the question-asking seed has been planted in her mind, and if it receives nurture, it may take root and stand firm against the flood of appeals to vanity, prejudice, and fear that threatens to engulf us all.

NOTES

For more information on any of the Appalshop programs cited contact Appalshop at 306 Madison Street, Whitesburg, Ky., 41858. The Appalshop School Initiative is supported by grants from the DeWitt Wallace–Reader's Digest Fund, the John D. and Catherine T. MacArthur Foundation, the BellSouth Foundation, and the Appalshop Production and Education Fund.

1. *The Mountain Eagle*, Whitesburg, Kentucky, May 15, 1991, p. B6; May 22, 1991, p. B8; June 12, 1991, p. B4.
2. "Man on Troublesome" is a production of Western Kentucky University Media Services. It was produced by Michael Lassiter. It is not an Appalshop production.

REFERENCES

Catfish: Man of the Woods, 1974. Film. Color, 27 min. Appalshop, Inc. Dir. Alan Bennett.
Man on Troublesome Creek, 1988. Film. Western Kentucky University Media Services. Dir. Michael Lassiter.
On Our Own Land, 1988. Film. Color, 29 min. Appalshop, Inc. Dir. Anne Johnson.
Portraits and Dreams, 1984. Video. Color and black-and-white, 17 min. Appalshop, Inc. Dir. Andrew Garrison with Wendy Ewald.
SMITH, HERB E., and HELEN LEWIS, 1984. Appalshop and the History of Appalachia. *Appalachian Journal* 11(Summer): 413.
STILL, JAMES, 1940. *River of Earth*. (Lexington: University Press of Kentucky).
Strangers and Kin: A History of the Hillbilly Image, 1984. Film. Color, 58 min. Appalshop, Inc. Dir. Herb E. Smith.

Bent, But Not Broken: Hurricane Hugo, Video, and Community-Centered Learning

Gail Matthews

Although statistics can depersonalize or sensationalize an experience, a few descriptive facts may help refresh the memories of those who may have forgotten the magnitude of Hurricane Hugo and its dramatic impact on local culture in the state of South Carolina. On September 21, 1989, the night of the hurricane, 135 mile-per-hour winds blew across the state, causing $10 million worth of damage per minute. About 1.3 million acres of trees were destroyed—approximately one-third of the state's commercial timber.

This pervasive material damage radically altered the cultural landscape of the state. Many residents of South Carolina discovered that their familiar surroundings suddenly appeared very foreign. Strangers in their own land, unable to find their way in territory that once was so familiar, the experience made many feel disoriented or even helpless.

Recollections of immediate reactions after the hurricane reveal a pervasive and intense disorientation. According to South Carolinian Nancy Bilton: "It was like, I don't live here! You know, this isn't my house! This isn't my town! I mean, it just didn't look like, it didn't look like where I lived. And there was nothing . . . everywhere you stepped, there was a tree! . . . You couldn't tell what was the driveway, what wasn't the driveway" (Hall, 1990).

Victims of the storm processed their extraordinary experiences through story swapping and the sharing of personal narratives. Informal storytelling among victims served many purposes: it acted as a conversational reality check; provided a periodic sense of relief during times of frustration; served as a conduit for newly discovered survival tips;

and helped community members reflect on the larger lessons that could be gleaned from this disaster. After such a traumatic event, storytelling helps people process their experiences, and gradually come to identify themselves as survivors rather than as victims. Through this process they eventually regain a sense of control or mastery over their own lives.

DISASTERS AND THE MEDIA

With its technological sophistication, the contemporary mass media tend to focus our national or international attention on disasters, creating an instant and enduring stereotype of a specific portion of the world at one highly unusual moment in time. News reports of outrageous personal-experience stories and photographs of agonized, unnamed faces in front of devastated houses etch the image of victims in our minds. As time passes, the media turn to other, more recent events, ignoring the victims' slow yet steady recovery from past misfortune— the physical and psychological rebuildings of individuals, communities, even states. Although it was tracked carefully by weather forecasts, Hurricane Hugo's impact on the state of South Carolina was much greater than anticipated, but only a few weeks after the storm, while South Carolina residents were still consumed by their initial trauma, a California earthquake eclipsed most of South Carolina's media attention.

In contrast with the national media depictions of Hurricane Hugo as a brief event in history, South Carolinians experienced this storm as a long, painful process that included advance preparation, the storm experience, a massive recovery effort, and subsequent reflection on lessons learned. The immediate experience of disaster entailed a face-to-face encounter with a force beyond human control and drove home the lesson that disasters are exercises in powerlessness (see also Danielson 1990).

Yet as time passed and the recovery process continued, healthy individuals met this challenge, experiencing a transformation from victim status into a self-identification as survivors, and finally, after substantial reflection, coming to see themselves as sage veterans of disaster (for more on stages of recovery after a traumatic event, see Ochberg 1988). As their self-identification gradually changed, their spoken lore about the disaster event and the role that this event had played in their lives was revised as well.

While the mass media are primarily concerned with the dramatic stories that disaster victims have to tell, cultural documentarians should not overlook the fascinating ongoing stories of those same people as they become survivors, as well as the insightful reflections that they have to offer as disaster veterans or experts. The following case study documents just such a project—a student-produced child's-eye view of Hurricane Hugo a year and a half after the storm.

OUR STORIES OF THE STORM: FOLKLORISTICS AND VIDEOGRAPHY IN PRIMARY EDUCATION

Realizing the importance of community dialogue and the expressive art of storytelling following a disaster, the South Carolina Arts Commission contacted the Folk Arts Program at the McKissick Museum of the University of South Carolina early in 1990 to consider a number of approaches that might help children process their experiences with Hurricane Hugo. The result was the "Our Stories of the Storm" project, an innovative video/folklore documentary project for school children in heavily damaged areas of South Carolina (Matthews 1991; Matthews and Patterson, 1991).

According to Scott Sanders (1990), executive director of the South Carolina Arts Commission, the objective of the project was to "help students, their families and their communities share their Hugo experiences and, in the process, find catharsis and reaffirmation that will contribute to their emotional and psychological recovery. We also hoped that this project would deliver a powerful, first-hand lesson to students and others about the value and importance of the arts and humanistic disciplines in their lives and in our society." "Our Stories of the Storm" received funding from the South Carolina Humanities Council, the National Endowment for the Arts, and the South Carolina Arts Commission. It was implemented as a cooperative venture of the Arts Commission and the Folk Arts Program.

After an initial training session for all adult participants developed in consultation with psychologists experienced in trauma therapy, a team comprised of one folklorist (the author) and one videographer traveled to two school sites and worked with the children in these schools to design their own videotaped statement about Hurricane Hugo. Each residency lasted three weeks.

During the school residencies, the children engaged in an initial orientation week of lessons designed to accomplish three sets of goals. First, creative group exercises gave the children basic training in question identification, interviewing, scriptwriting, and the technical knowledge necessary to operate High-8 and Super-VHS cameras. Second, instructors helped the children examine their notion of history. Many of the students believed that history only described and theorized about events in the distant past. The lessons helped students come to understand that they had lived through an important historical event, had a first-hand expertise regarding hurricanes, and were therefore well equipped to act as historians documenting their community's experience. During this time the students were also encouraged to tell their own personal Hugo stories and reflect on their experiences. Finally, the class examined the whole notion of storytelling—why stories are told and the many possible art forms that can tell stories (for example, dance, puppetry, song, even video itself).

At the end of the first week, the children were asked to decide how they wanted to tell their collective Hurricane Hugo story on videotape. The children in both groups related their story by taping a variety of short vignettes, editing them together to create a longer finished piece. Interviews with community members, group-authored rap songs, images of damaged buildings, drawings with narrated description, and puppet shows were some of the pieces that they videotaped.

Although the children often related vivid and frightening stories about their hurricane experiences in class, they decided that they wanted their final videotape to be primarily an affirmation of their survival. One class even wanted to conclude their videotape with a survivors' party, complete with helium-filled balloons. As mentioned earlier, after a disaster local residents are usually identified by the media as "victims." Initially this label is not a problem because the residents in a disaster area do genuinely feel like victims. However, this "victim" label can become problematic over time, especially for communities that work very hard to recover. Outsiders, remembering those powerful media images of destruction, may still think of these people as victims, while the people themselves have progressed beyond this label. The "Our Stories of the

Storm" school residencies occurred one year after the storm, by which time many South Carolinians had been able to recover and reflect and were ready to view their past trauma in the most positive light.

REFLECTIONS ON PROJECT STRUCTURE

In reviewing the results of these school residencies, certain features in project design appear to be crucial to successful student video projects. Student empowerment was of primary concern in this project. The children needed to know that the instructors genuinely wanted to learn their story as only they would tell it. Our experience suggests that it is crucial for the children to have complete control over the editing and scripting decisions and for them to perform most, if not all, of the videotaping and editing. To accommodate this need for student control, we feel that the optimum length for this kind of project would be four weeks, rather than three.

This project is similar to Sol Worth and John Adair's *Through Navajo Eyes* (1972), in which Navajo Indians were given cameras and allowed to create their own statements about their life and culture. The "Our Stories" project contrasted with the Navajo project in its orientation phase. Instead of handing the children cameras and sending them out into their community to make untutored videotapes, we provided some initial training in folklore, history, interviewing techniques, and videography. In that training we undoubtedly oriented them to certain documentary conventions. However, "purity" is questionable in either case because a basic level of technical skills is needed to translate successfully images that a documentarian has in his or her head onto film or video. Projects concerned with seeing through the eyes of "the other" are caught in an interesting paradox. Project initiators have a choice either of giving group members video equipment without instruction, knowing that they may lack certain technical skills necessary to communicate their insider's perspective in that medium, or of working with the group first to help them attain certain documentary skills and knowing that in this educational process the group is being influenced by the semiotic system of another culture.

Another challenge that the instructors for this project faced was setting aside their own documentary and artistic egos. A project like this takes the folklorist and the videographer out of the driver's seat and sets the traditional relationship between documentor and subject on its head. This inversion can present some problems for most cultural documentarians accustomed to creating their own statements about the cultures that they encounter. The goal of allowing a group of children to find their own voice is deceptively simple. The instructor, as an adult, outsider, and social scientist, may consider some of the footage that winds up on the cutting room floor priceless. The class may decide to edit these scenes out because this footage does not express the message that they want or it does not coincide with the children's desired presentation of self.

The school residencies worked best when the folklorist and videographer acted as facilitators, rather than primary researchers or media artists, and helped the children design and execute all aspects of their project on their own. In order to achieve a good student/teacher ratio, one residency divided up the class into three production teams consisting of about six students. Each team had a designated producer, director, audio technician, camera operator, and talent. Although the producer and director roles were fixed, other team members changed jobs from shoot to shoot as needed.

After some initial concern that the children might inadvertently damage the video equipment, we found that the children inevitably treated the equipment with respect if they were taught its value and how to handle it with care. We also discovered that children in low-income communities responded especially well to working with professional video equipment on an in-depth project. All of the children were anxious to work on something "real" and were enthusiastic about being taken seriously as cultural documentarians.

This hands-on, experiential orientation to video in the classroom transforms traditional notions of video-as-product into one of video-as-process. In contrast with adults, who usually cannot wait until the film is developed or the video is played back, children demonstrate more interest in the moment of documentation, often not even asking to see the resulting photographic prints or video. We discovered that the most important aspect of the project was the experience: the process of helping the children decide how they wanted to relate their story; the analyti-

Videographer Don Patterson helps a Mayesville, South Carolina, elementary school student learn how to operate a video camera. Other students and Gail Matthews look on.

Mayesville elementary school rap group.

cal discoveries that the children made as they critiqued their own work; and the rapport that developed between the children, their teachers, the video-folklore facilitator team, and the larger community.

We believe that this fortuitous combination of video and folklore in the classroom has tremendous potential beyond our work with hurricane stories. Similar projects could help students create videotapes about pressing social issues, local lore, or just about any other topic. Imagine projects that encourage students to go out into their communities, interviewing people about their experiences and feelings. This use of video encourages the entire community to participate in the educational process and advocates an educational model in which learning is truly a part of everyday life.

REFLECTIONS ON VIDEO CONTENT

My presentation of an "Our Stories of the Storm" student video to the Southern Anthropological Society during the 1991 Key Symposium required me to move out of my role as the nurturing-but-neutral project facilitator, and attempt to assume a more analytical perspective in order to reflect on what I had learned about children and disaster survivors. I must admit that this shift was extremely difficult. When I show the video to adults I am often caught by surprise when they laugh at portions of the piece that I know the children took very seriously. No half-hour video can communicate the transformation that I saw take place in the children during this project. With these limitations in mind, I have wrestled a few observations from my academic self.

Common Video Themes

The most common theme in the student video is that of power and powerlessness. Pictures that the children drew of the hurricane depict it as an anthropomorphized black funnel cloud, complete with ominous facial features. One skit shows children who are frightened off by "Hugo," who plays the role of a bully dressed in black while they are chanting and dancing a Hugo rap. In this rap sequence, the hurricane is so "bad" (in a contemporary colloquial sense) that its power inspires a form of awe-based admiration. However, in the following group-authored rap lyrics, the children declare that they are even tougher than the storm because of their ability to become survivors:

> Here's a little story that we have to tell
> about some people who weren't aware.
> The hurricane came without delay—
> destroyed everything in its way.
> Hurricane Hugo was a bad storm,
> he made some people feel alone.
> But we are survivors as you can see.
> We made this rap for you and me.
> Peace!

This pride in being "badder" than the storm is also reflected in a group photo that the children took of their rap group (p. 152).

This attention to the dark side of power is countered by the many interviews with community role models that are prominently featured in the piece, including interviews with the principal, local church deacons, and even the district school superintendent. During the interviews the children looked to these adults for commentary on how the community dealt with the hurricane. They were also very curious about how these powerful adults felt during and after the storm. They seemed to be looking to these adults for permission to feel fear and openly acknowledge any anxieties that they might have felt during the storm.

Another theme the students grappled with in many scenes of their video was the dissolution of order. One student stood in front of a completely demolished building and explained that it had been her friend's house and that everything that the friend had put away "nicely and neatly" had been destroyed. Time and time again, I had the impression that the disorder was as devastating as the destruction for many of the children. Likewise, a construction paper model that the students built to reenact the hurricane stressed the orderliness of their lives before the wind came and rearranged their town.

Narrative Conventions

In reviewing the students' video, I realize that there is an unusual and interesting narrative convention at work. Instead of telling their story chronologically, from disaster to recovery, the students begin their video with affirmations of survival. As the video opens four or five chil-

Mayesville elementary school student interviews the district school superintendent. Positive role models were prominently featured in the student video.

The students focused on the disorder associated with Hurricane Hugo. Here students examine the remains of a friend's house as they scout locations to shoot.

dren run, one at a time, in front of the camera and shout, "My name is ———, and I am a survivor of Hurricane Hugo." The video then cuts to a group shot in the classroom during which the children shout, "We are all survivors of Hurricane Hugo." They begin with a celebration of survival, then fill in more details about their trauma in bits and pieces. If the video were chronologically organized, the viewer would first see the community's weak side, the victim side. While beginning the video with scenes of disaster and destruction might build empathy for the students and their community, this is not the effect that the children desired. Opening with dramatic depictions of the storm is more in keeping with the victim-oriented conventions of mass media.

The children told me that they wanted people all over the country to see their video, if possible. They wanted to share what they had learned about survival with others. These children began their video with the "survivor" material because this is how they first want to be seen by the outside, unknown world. For them the hurricane experience was a disturbing story that could be tolerated only if the viewer knew that it had a good ending.

As the video progresses, viewers piece together, often by inference, the story that these children have to tell. Bits and pieces add up to a cumulative sense of narrative—we filter the many scenes through our own understanding and therefore create our own documentary. This understanding is not monolithic; it changes for me with each screening and is undoubtedly also different for each viewer.

Presentation of Self

After viewing an initial rough edit of the video, the South Carolina Arts Commission assistant deputy director Ken May remarked that, in his opinion, the video was missing the kinds of "stories" that he had expected: whole houses destroyed while china tea sets remained perfectly intact; eerie and detailed descriptions of the eye of the storm; individuals who miraculously survived while crouched in seemingly unprotected places. When I thought on this comment, I tended to agree with Ken. During the spring semester after the storm my university class had collected a number of amazing stories that would make good copy in any newspaper. During my residency with the elementary students, they also told some amazing stories: seeing a human face in the eye of the storm; a bicycle miraculously and safely chained to a post despite the fact that the entire surrounding garage was destroyed; people seen stuck in trees. Yet the children made many editing decisions that surprised me, cutting out these stories and other details that I thought were the "good stuff." Instead, the final piece was highly promotional in effect, complete with a school commercial and endorsements by community leaders.

The more I thought about my fascination as an outsider with the colorful stories that are usually associated with the initial "victim" stage after a disaster, the more I was confronted with my own need to play the role of the benevolent "rescuer" who goes into disadvantaged areas and returns with exotic stories to tell. While the help of outsiders was undoubtedly crucial to physical and material recovery after the hurricane, the most notable and growth-producing experiences for these children involved their own personal, family, and community activities. They wanted to tell the world about their own active participation in their recovery. This highly disruptive experience had provided an opportunity for growth; for example, an interview with the father of one of the students highlighted the fact that although his auto repair garage was destroyed by the storm the replacement garage he was building would be better than the one before the storm. His garage construction site had become a gathering place for the entire community—a place to chat while they inspected each day's progress.

In this student video we see glimpses of interior life but are never invited to enter. Common social scientific documentary conventions involve probing the inner life of the subject, entering what we consider to be the interior world of "the other." In this instance, "the other" decides how much of the community's interior life will be shown to the outside world and chooses to excise personal experience narratives.

FINAL QUESTIONS

In conclusion, this project leaves me with a number of unresolved questions, some of which are specific to this particular residency, some of which would apply to any community video project. First, the school residency in which I participated took place with an entirely African-American student population. It is a common practice in southeastern

African-American communities to ask role models to testify at public events (for example, school reunions, choir anniversaries, local festivals, church revivals). To what extent is the prominent featuring of church deacons, teachers, and other powerful members of the community a documentary convention associated with African-American culture?

My residency also took place in an economically disadvantaged community. To what extent do economic factors, coupled with a desire for dignity, influence editorial decisions? If the summer home of an individual with no experience of poverty is destroyed, the image of their home in ruins will not summon up any preexisting memories of poverty. In contrast, if a person of limited financial resources has worked very hard for years to attain a standard of living in adulthood only dreamed of in childhood, the disarray following a disaster could resonate with unpleasant memories and have a very different effect. There may be issues of pride and dignity at play when a lower socioeconomic group documents its own community following a disaster that the privileged may not be able to fathom.

Finally, there is a question of time. This documentation project occurred more than a year after the storm. Writings on post-traumatic stress indicate that there is a process of identity renegotiation that begins following the trauma with an immediate sense of self-as-victim and progressing to a sense of self-as-survivor. Would these children have made a different video statement about their experience if the project had taken place one year earlier? I am fairly certain that the video would have been entirely different. This possibility calls into question our whole notion of history, indicating that the story of what happened, our story of the event, our sense of ourselves and our role in that event, and even our historical reality change as time progresses.

NOTE

Upon completing this project, the residency lesson plans were revised into a more general class curriculum entitled *Learning from Your Community: Folklore and Video in the Classroom* (Matthews and Patterson 1991) that can be used by educators in planning and implementing similar projects. An edited videotape curriculum companion depicts the preparatory lessons aimed at helping children acquire documentary and video skills. For more information about this curriculum package, contact the Media Arts Center, South Carolina Arts Commission, 1800 Gervais Street, Columbia, S.C. 29201-3585.

REFERENCES

DANIELSON, LARRY, 1990. Tornado Stories in the Breadbasket: Weather and Regional Identity. In *Sense of Place: American Regional Cultures*, Barbara Allen and Thomas J. Schlereth, eds. (Lexington: University Press of Kentucky).

HALL, KATHERINE, 1990. Interview with Nancy Bilton, March. Unpublished collection project for USC Honors College American Folklore class. Transcript archived at the South Carolina Folk Arts Program Archive, McKissick Museum, University of South Carolina, Columbia.

MATTHEWS, GAIL, 1991. Video and Folklore in the Classroom. *Independent Spirit* 12 (2) : 2–3.

MATTHEWS, GAIL, and DON PATTERSON, 1991. *Learning from Your Community: Folklore and Video in the Schools. A Classroom Curriculum for Grades 4–8* (Columbia: South Carolina Arts Commission).

OCHBERG, FRANK, ed., 1988. *Post-Traumatic Therapy and Victims of Violence* (New York: Brunner/Marzel).

SANDERS, SCOTT, 1990. Letter to school personnel.

WORTH, SOL, and JOHN ADAIR, 1972. *Through Navajo Eyes: An Exploration in Film Communication in Anthropology* (Bloomington: Indiana University Press).

PART 4
On Snakes and People

"Bizarre Snake Handlers": Popular Media and a Southern Stereotype

Jim Birckhead

The last time I saw "snake handling" was in the winter of 1986 in the small town of Deniliquin, perched at the edge of "the great Australian outback" in the western New South Wales mallee country, about as far away from the American South as one could be.[1] The occasion was not a religious service, or even a carnival, but the performance of Jane Martin's play *Talking With* . . . (1983) by a theater company from Wagga Wagga known for its high-quality productions of modern and experimental plays.

I had made the two-hour drive from home on this bleak, rainy night to "see" the play because my amazed students (and a posted handbill advertising "comedy with a sting in its tail") had informed me that one of its vignettes, "Handler," portrayed a Holiness woman and featured the actress handling on stage a nonpoisonous snake named Fang.

Given my long-term interest in the construction of dramatic, fictional, filmic, media, and ethnographic representations of Pentecostal-Holiness serpent handlers (I once attended a literary luncheon in Canberra to talk with Lisa Alther about her sources of inspiration for Clem Cloyd, the serpent handler in *Kinflicks* [1977]), I was rewarded by the transparency of the event; the play itself, its performance, and audience reaction all revealed the workings of popular typifications and stereotypes about "the South."

Huddled under a blanket with a grazier and his wife in the barely heated, cavernous, and cold former town hall that now served as the venue for traveling theater, and sharing this space with the couple of dozen or so keen theater-goers, I gazed with stunned attention and post-modern bemusement as the young actress in a hackneyed southern accent cutely and seductively performed a parodic rendition of Caro, the "Handler" (Martin 1983:49–50):

My Dada [pronounced "Dad-aw"] was gonna do this tonight but the Lord froze his face so he sent me. I learned this from my Dada and he learned it up from Gran, who took it on from the Reverend Soloman Bracewood, who had him a mule ministry 'round these parts way back when. Dada taught Miss Ellie, my ma, and my brother Jamie . . . he was in it too, 'fore he went for Detroit.

See, what I got in here is snakes. Lotta people don't like snakes. Gives it its nature, I guess. This here is water mocs, Jamie, he said they got the dirtiest, nastiest bite of all . . . well, rattlers is yer biggest. Lotta venom. You milk you a rattler, you can half fill up a juice glass. Dada said Jamie should do rattlers, but he never. Did 'heads, copperheads. Now they're slower and safer but it ain't such a good show. You know those dang snakes smell like cucumbers? Well, they do. Miss Ellie, she favored moccasins. Dada too . . . well, Dada he did all kinds, all ways. Your moccasin now, he's your good ol' boy snake. Flat out mean an' lots of get up n' go. Heck, they'll chase ya. They will. Ol' Dada he didn't like Miss Ellie doin' 'em. "You lay off them mocs 'fore they lay you down." Made Miss Ellie laugh. Lotta handlers think moccasins are slimy. Couldn't get me to touch one. They'll do rattlers . . . got him a nice dry feel. Little bit sandpapery. Rattler can find ya in the pitch dark though. They git on to yer body heat. Snake handlin'. *All* my blood does it. Only Dada an' me now though. Snake handlin', with the Holiness Church. Down where I come from we take God pretty serious. If you got the spirit, snake don't bite. If he bites you, you know you ain't got the spirit. Makes the difference real clear, don't it?

It's right there in the scripture . . . Mark, Chapter 16, verses 17 and 18, "And these signs shall follow them that believe. In my name they shall cast out devils; they shall speak in new tongues; they shall take up serpents; and if they drink any deadly thing, it shall not hurt them; they shall lay hands on the sick and they shall recover." Don't figure it could be much clearer than that. There's some churches don't use snakes, use strychnine, powdered poison, same idea though. They mix it with cherry Kool-aid, sing 'em a hymn, drink it off, and then just stand around waitin' to see if they fall over. Ain't much of a show. Not like snakes. Dada does fire but I can't do it. Pours some kerosene in a coke bottle, sticks a rag in the top and lights it up. Holds that fire under his chin, passes it down the arm, puts his hand in it, you know, that kind of stuff. He says there's people do blow torches down to Tennessee. I don't know. Jamie give it a try 'fore he went to Detroit. Just about burned his ass off. Sorry. . . . [2]

By intermission, news of my presence had passed through the audience, such as it was, and I had become a minor celebrity for the evening. I had driven all the way from Albury just to see this strange "American" play and had been to Appalachia and seen first-hand people handling snakes in church: "What is it really like?" "Are snake handlers inbred like in *Deliverance*?" "How backward are they?"

After the performance I asked the director and the actress who played Caro about their "reading" of the character and how they constructed the portrayal. They had not, it seemed, been able to find any literature on Holiness people and had fabricated the characterization from popularly held images and stereotypes of stock Appalachian and southern types. The role was modeled largely on filmic and media images of the South, especially *Deliverance*, which conjured up for them lurid images of bizarre, grotesque, inbred "hillbillies." The actress's intuitive sense of Caro had led her to project an affective tone of "extreme fanaticism and sexuality."

My thoughts drifted back to the "dogwood winter" day in April 1973, when I attended Brother Buford's funeral in Madison County, North Carolina. Bu, and Jimmy, had died of strychnine consumed during a church service in Tennessee. The graveside mood was somber and full of shock and disbelief that this had happened to two "saints" of the church. Serpents were taken up in the graveyard, a group affirmation of faith and community. (In fact, to elude the sheriff I had transported the snakes myself to and from the cemetery in a Volkswagen "beetle.")

I found the juxtaposition of images jarring—"precious memories" of 1973 Holiness Appalachia and 1986 Deniliquin post-performance discourse of parody, amusement, and stereotype. I could not reconcile the staged representation of the one-dimensional Caro with the warmth, individuality, and sanity of my Holiness friends, who very little resemble the bizarre character I had seen portrayed on stage. The Holiness people of my experience are three-dimensional and inhabit an everyday world of human needs, feelings, and individual aspirations.

In a lighter vein, I recalled evenings in the basement of the hillside church, sitting with brothers and sisters and laughing at *Hustler* galley proofs, the latest newspaper or television portrayal of the church, or anticipating the imminent arrival of a BBC reporter and film crew. (Or, stepping out of this text for a moment, the incredulous laughter of Holiness women at the portrayal in *Talking With* . . . .)

But, the image of serpent handlers comically and critically "reading" a *Hustler* galley proof or the script of a play like *Talking With* . . . or "deconstructing" videotape documentaries about themselves is jarring as well, as we do not expect such people to be so reflexive. This is, after all, inconsistent with the illiterate, southern, backwoods, crazed religious fanatic of popular stereotype; a set of images that have been developed over a number of years and in many genres—images that obviously were very much a part of popular consciousness twelve thousand miles from Tennessee in western New South Wales, Australia, on a winter's night in 1986.

"MOUNTAIN VOODOO": POSITIONING "SNAKE HANDLERS"[3]

Although small in number of churches and adherents, the Pentecostal-Holiness religion, "with signs following," has been extremely "newsworthy" since its obscure origins in east Tennessee in the early 1900s. Print, photographic, and television journalists, as well as playwrights, fiction writers, documentary filmmakers, and, to a lesser degree, social scientists, have produced a plethora of images of these "bizarre," "shocking," and "primitive" religious practices of "white," "Anglo-Saxon" southerners (see McNeil 1989:285).

The production and availability of such images has waxed and waned over the years, depending upon the number of snakebite or poison victims (and the ensuing legal prosecution), the tenor of the times, and the sheer hunger of popular media for page-three, tabloid, or television news-magazine human interest features. That "snake handling" has lent itself so well to media image making is not surprising. The snake has long served as a powerful and disturbing symbol, repelling yet tantalizing; evoking dark suggestions of satanic evil and death, and titillatingly linked with phallic eroticism and immortality. Not only is the snake an evocative multivocal symbol, it is almost universally feared and reviled. Snake stories are very much a part of folklore and popular culture. This is especially true of "good old boy" adventure and hunting narratives of rattlesnake roundups and of the manly prowess of secular snake handlers who perform in the liminal world of carnivals and traveling snake shows in the South. Given such discourses about snakes, images of southern "whites" handling snakes and fire and drinking poisons in the name of religion are potent and marketable commodities indeed.

Due to space limitations, I will not examine in detail the full range of popular media representations of serpent handling. Rather, I focus on

"Intertextuality." At a vacant used car lot near Knoxville, Tennessee, a "snake handler" and a Holiness serpent handler stand in front of snake show billboard. The image in the bottom right-hand corner was inspired by the serpent handler.

images of serpent handling on television, especially foreign news magazine productions, as these short "documentaries" reveal in bold relief the cinemagraphic and narrative conventions that construct for a mass audience, often during prime time, this "bizarre" corner of the "mythic South" (Tindall 1989:1097).

Yet, I cannot avoid making at least some reference to print and photographic coverage of serpent handling, as these have established in part widely held commonsense notions of what this reality is like (see Maggard 1983–84) and the larger regional stereotypes such notions feed into and help construct. Indeed, this television genre derives much of "its narrative form, its representational codes, and its structure of looking" from these other media (Clark 1990:118). Namely, such stories appear to be dominated by a heavy voice-over narrative line, catchy "headlines," and a style, structure of presentation, and visual grammar that conform to codes of "journalistic logic" (Langer 1980:17).

Within these conventions, popular narrative and visual representations have created a standard "look" for "snake handlers" that positions "them" as very much "other" to "us"; as spectacle or carnival sideshow, part of "believe it or not," bizarre adventure genres, the objects of our voyeuristic media gaze. We characteristically peer up or straight ahead at a "snake handler," who characteristically is portrayed with mouth agape exposing teeth, nostrils flared, face contorted, long straggly hair (on women) hanging down, eyes wild and glazed, grasping a snake or snakes with exaggerated fingers and knuckles at the end of long outstretched arms thrust into the foreground.

The "otherness" of serpent handlers is further accentuated by the use of archival and file photos (and footage) in some pieces such as the "snake handlers" entry in the *Encyclopedia of Southern Culture* (Wilson and Ferris 1989:1330), which includes an old photo captioned "Snake handlers of eastern Tennessee, date unknown." The dress and hairstyles worn, background settings, and general "look" serve to position "them" as "old timey," archaic, not part of the contemporary world. In many such examples, the handlers remain anonymous and the dates are not provided, contributing to a stereotypical, natural history–like viewing of specimens similar to the positioning of indigenous "others" as exemplified by postcard portraits—for example, "Aboriginals, Northern Territory. Reputed to be one of the most primitive races in the world, these aborigines perform an ancient and picturesque ceremony."

Photographs, old and recent, are usually stark assemblages in sharp black-and-white, highlighting angular featured people beneath naked light bulbs. An eerie effect is produced by camera shots of handlers' heads partially obscuring unshaded bulbs, creating an elongated halo of bright light. Photos showing people drinking poison or handling fire are similarly constructed and often include other participants exhibiting various degrees of "crazed" behaviors. I have a number of such framed eight-by-ten shots taken by photographers on my office wall and am haunted by these fixed images of people I have known for many years (some now dead) peering at me like mounted museum displays.

These frozen moments of captured ecstasy have become icons of Holiness religion. Lifted from the context of everyday life and religious practice, such typifications amplify and distort the meaning, frequency, number of participants, and duration of serpent handling, fire handling, and drinking of "deadly things." Thus, although serpent handling is not practiced by all members, does not occur during every church service, takes place as infrequently as once a year in some congregations, may last no longer than five minutes of a four-hour service, and is embedded in a sophisticated system of meaning, the iconic image has come to signify an entire group of relatively diverse individuals and practices in rather distorted and stereotypical ways. And acting on the mistaken assumption that "the camera does not lie," we fail to realize that "photography's relationship with reality is as tenuous as that of any other medium" (Ritchin 1990:1). For as Fred Ritchin (1990:1) notes further, "The common error is to confuse, in the stasis, and apparent certitude of visual realism, the representation with the thing itself; the frozen instant, the slice from space with the more fluid, interconnected life to which it merely refers."

Such photographic images are further contextualized as bizarre, trivial, or comic by the headlines, titles, and captions used in the article or story in which they appear. For example, a one page piece in *Globe* (July 26, 1983), "The Gospel of Death," proclaims in bold print, "Congregations play with snakes, fire and even drink poisons." It further positions the people more specifically in slightly smaller bold print: "A bizarre religious sect praises the Lord by handling poisonous snakes, putting fire on their bodies and drinking deadly poisons." The reader is gratified by the inclusion of three photos that display these behaviors. The first shows a participant holding a handful of serpents in the standard pose described earlier; the caption reads: "This worshipper was bitten moments after this picture was taken. But, amazingly, the very next day he was handling snakes again." The second frame depicts a man's head in profile with jutting chin and tongue extended into the flames of a torch, with the caption: "Sizemore's burning faith: 'They thought Jesus was crazy too.'" The third shows a shoulders-up profile of a woman drinking from a large jar: "Deadly concoction: these people are afraid of nothing."

The following headlines reflect graphically the popular journalistic construction of "snake handlers":

Holiness Splinter Sects: Reincarnation, Polygamy and Snakes (*Los Angeles Times*, April 29, 1973)

Snake Church—An Appalachian Sect Praises the Lord and Passes the Copperheads (*US*, July 18, 1983)

Serpent Handling Churches Still Exist in the Deep South (*Edmonton Journal*, December 18, 1971)

Fangs Fatal to Georgia Carpenter—Snake Handling Still Widespread (*The Tennessean*, December 31, 1972)

Snake Handler Convention—Ecstasy with a Deadly Cobra (*Atlanta Constitution*, July 2, 1973)

Cultist Shrugs Off Rattlesnake Bite (*Los Angeles Times*, July 2, 1973)

Rattlesnake Strikes Chattanooga Fondler (*Knoxville Journal*, July 2, 1973)

A Preacher's Date with Death (*Edmonton Journal*, June 15, 1974)

"No Need to Let Left Hand Know"—Right One Holds Hissing Copperhead (*Knoxville Journal*, June 21, 1973)

Ministers Kill Selves (*Knoxville Journal*, April 9, 1973)

Two Dead from Poison—Religious Cult to Add Test of Faith by Fire (*Los Angeles Times*, April 14, 1973)

Snakes Handled at Two Burials (*Knoxville News Sentinel*, April 12, 1973)

"They Shall Take Up Serpents"—The Salvation of Suffering Technology Can't Stop (*St. Louis Post Dispatch*, March 18, 1987)

The South—Paralyzing Prayers (*Time* 46, no. 12, September 17, 1945), pp. 23–24

On T.V. Show—Pastor Holds Snake Despite Injunction (*Knoxville News Sentinel*, July 30, 1973)

Holy Snakes (promotional review for a BBC-produced film, *They Shall Take Up Serpents*, 1985).

More often than not, the texts of such stories are crowded with descriptors like "bizarre," "weird," "zany," "crazy," "frenzied," "lunatic fringe," and implicit and explicit suggestions of hillbilly moonshining, inbreeding, and low intelligence. Even more lurid and shocking portrayals occur in fictional, semifictional, and dramatic works on serpent handling that contain their share of backwoods bearded patriarchs; "toothless crones"; gaunt, barefoot, longhaired, sweating, gyrating (even bare-breasted) young Holiness sisters; love feasts of rattlesnake meat and moonshine; vivid descriptions of bloody snakebites and death; and truly fantastic descriptions of madness and confusion, sexuality and fanaticism, and general grotesqueness—as fitting many examples of southern Gothic writing (see Gossett 1965).

All told, images of "snake handling," although sporadic, fragmentary, and fleeting, nonetheless, have been disseminated worldwide over many years and have become a peripheral part of popular culture and consciousness if only as a dimly imagined awareness people have of the existence of "a cult of crazy hillbilly snake charmers" frozen in archaic time somewhere in the mythic geography of the American Bible Belt in the remote South. Following up a point made by Edward Said about the diversity of Islam, the very erudite host of the Australian Broadcasting Corporation (ABC) Radio National current affairs and arts program "Late Night Live" commented (February 6, 1991) that Christianity, like Islam, "covers a multitude of sins and virtues from Deep Southern rattlesnake wrestling to the lofty theologizing of a Hans Küng." The responses of most people upon learning that I have studied serpent handling are similarly uninformed. But almost everyone of my acquaintance has heard of it and knows that it takes place in "the South." This "cult" of popular imagination, from my experience, also is tinged with resonances of *Deliverance* and the suicides at Jonestown.

Given the tone of popular media representations, and I might add some scholarly and documentary texts as well, the question can be asked: Who are these people and how can we know them? What kind of "vantage point" (Bakhtin 1991:25) do our standard discourses afford us in "seeing" (Berger 1972) people who engage in such culturally and socially ungrammatical practices? How does one textualize such people without making it read like caricature and lampoon (see Darnell 1991)?

In this regard I have often been mildly shocked by my university students who characteristically laugh during the documentary film *Chase the Devil* when the somber voiced narrator reports that the snakebite victim recovered, although Jimmy, the spokesman, later died from drinking strychnine. Why do they laugh at such a sad and serious event? Do they really lack human feelings? I suspect not. Rather, serpent handling, not unlike the suicides at Jonestown (Drummond 1983:172), has been so completely structured as a journalistic and media event that it is "read" as parody and fiction having little or nothing to do with real human beings in a real world.[4] And, like Jonestown, serpent handling religion has generated little ethnographic work. Jonestown, Drummond (1983:172–73) suggests, was more or less ignored by ethnographers because of "the event's sensationalism and its ugliness.... The Jonestown massacres/suicides are a specifically nonethnographic event for them because they were so bizarre and so modern.... We begin and end our studies by asking the native to be beautiful and whole. But what if he is deformed and self-destructive? That is the question Jonestown poses."

I have felt for a long time that many anthropologists hold similar attitudes about serpent handling as a serious topic of research. Over the past twenty years I have presented in four countries a number of papers on this religion, and despite my efforts at serious analysis, I have been amazed at the number of questions of a prurient or frivolous nature; questions and preoccupations structured more by journalistic than by ethnographic discourses: "Are they inbred?" "How similar are they to the people in *Deliverance*?" "What kind of snakes do they use?"—even when this information was given in the paper. Often, to my dismay, time for questions following a paper is taken up with this sort of spurious concern to the detriment of serious discussion of the cultural and social meanings of serpent handling and its place in Appalachian culture. That these people were seen as southerners, "rednecks," "hillbillies," poor whites, I suspect, biases even anthropological readings of this "culture," causing the rules of relativism to be suspended. Had these practices occurred among black or indigenous Americans, Papuan New Guineans, or aboriginal Australians, I have often thought, the topic would be afforded greater interest and seriousness and, therefore, respect for its participants as part of humanity.

While serpent handling has not been studied extensively by ethnographers, its over-representation by the popular media is phenomenal, to the extent that the "snake handler" has emerged as an icon of Appalachian and southern "otherness." Recent critiques of portrayals of Appalachia decry this situation. Curtis Seltzer (1978:134), for example, notes that "the news picture of the illiterate, gun-happy, snake-handling, Appalachian mutant of the Angles and the Saxons lacks fairness, accuracy and truth." Similarly, David Whisnant (1979:5–8) in writing about the Appalachian stereotype states that "the accompanying text will usually set these picturesque artifacts in an appropriate context of folkways and convoluted kinship systems, Elizabethan speech patterns, resistance to modernity, and a stern and fatalistic religion that veers tantalizingly toward snake-handling."

William McNeil (1977:63), with respect to folklore scholarship, offers the opinion that "too often public interest in Appalachia has focused on curious or fringe groups and, of these, perhaps none have received more publicity than the literalists churches that practice snake-handling." Finally, Mauer (1978:1) writes: "To fit the popular stereotype of Appalachia, over exposure is frequently accorded by the mass media to the more unusual religious groups such as the serpent handlers." (Maggard, 1983–84, makes a similar point.)

My own ethnographic site in east Tennessee, near a town once dubbed by the media as "the snakehandling capital of the world" (Fortunato 1980:52), graphically illustrates the intense media fascination with serpent handling. First of all, I should make it clear that I did not set out in 1971 to study the media representation of Holiness serpent handling. Indeed, I had not yet heard of "representation," let alone "a crisis in representation," and as an ethnographer in the "realist tradition" I had intended to describe a "culture" out there where the locals "still do it." Proceeding from studies of the time, I conceived this group to be relatively isolated, "traditional," and quintessentially Appalachian; to study "them" would not be problematic, as it would be largely an exercise of data collection to be fitted into tried and true functionalist or interactionist paradigms.

The pervasiveness of media coverage of this small church, however, compelled me to look at this very visible aspect of community life and to become skeptical of notions of isolation, reputed secretiveness, and essential Appalachian character. Ironically, my initial contact with this church resulted from a newspaper account and photograph of a bitten handler, and on my first foray into "snake hollow" I was greeted by the sight of a free-lance photographer clicking away frames of serpent handling—a sight I was to see often at this church.

Indeed, this small congregation of some twenty to fifty people was featured in three documentary films and two video documentaries. They also were the subject of television news-magazine productions by the Canadian Broadcasting Corporation (CBC), "Wake Up America," and the British Broadcasting Corporation (BBC), and of some seventy-five newspaper stories, two popular books, chapters in books on exorcism, a photographic book on Appalachian people, and a Ph.D. dissertation. They appeared in numerous national magazines, and individuals in the church appeared (and handled snakes) on television talk shows and on local, regional, and national radio broadcasts.

As this is one congregation of less than fifty people, I am amused by the fiction constructed by the realist media that "snake handling cultists" are isolated and secretive but that somehow this or that reporter or film crew gained rare access for the first time. I will now examine realist media's representation of serpent handling on television.

"THIRD WORLD MUSIC"—"SNAKE HANDLERS" ON TELEVISION

Although serpent handling has been covered extensively by popular print media, its most evocative and graphic portrayal is found on documentary film and television. As I have suggested before, television and most documentary film representations of this religion draw heavily on journalistic meaning, codes, and conventions that have constructed these people as trivial and bizarre objects of our sensationalistic gaze.

Much of the texture of such portrayals derives from the presumed location of these people in "hillbilly-land" (Maggard 1983–84:72) with all its wider mythic connotations. As Horace Newcomb (1979–80:155) observes with respect to the Appalachian stereotype on television: "Even those viewers who have little idea of the true boundaries of the region, know a 'hillbilly' when they see one and immediately create the full symbolic context in which the image is 'supposed' to appear," the subtext of which structures the perception that "hillbilly ain't beautiful" (Branscome 1971:25).

As a full discussion of documentary film is beyond the scope of this paper (see Clements 1977 and 1979), I will now focus on television portrayals of serpent handling, especially news-magazine features; I will comment on documentaries only when they occur on television and take on added meanings from this medium.

Images of serpent handling appear sporadically and infrequently on television. Apart from the odd documentary broadcast as part of a series about culture and religion in general, short news items about injury or death by snakebite, or incidentally as part of a larger documentary about Appalachia, the South, or snakes, most stories of "snake handling" are screened as three- to ten-minute popular news magazine features on morning programs, "Sixty Minutes," and post–evening news public affairs formats.

Television news-magazine "documentaries" on serpent handlers, if not most coverage of this religion, share key features with what John Langer (1980:13–14) calls the "other news," stories that are not considered to be part of the "serious" news. Such stories "are relegated to a residual category, and are set aside as the 'lighter items,' the 'non-news' " or "news that has no value, a kind of anti-news" (Connell 1977:200) that is "signified by its 'triviality' and marginality to 'real' events" (Langer 1980:13–14).

Langer takes exception to the view that so-called serious news "represents political reality and culture more directly and significantly than the latter [other news]" (1980:14). Namely, all news is a cultural product, a construction, a "created reality" (Nimmo and Combs 1985:7), involving selectivity, genre conventions, and an ethos, and is controlled and produced by large media corporations and networks. Thus, "television news is not 'a neutral image' of reality or a 'window on the world' as professional newsmakers would have us believe" (Langer 1980:13) and therefore can be deconstructed to reveal its mythic and ideological functions in constructing and reproducing "the dominant meaning system and models of society: . . . how it constructs images of society by actively ruling in and ruling out certain realities." Seen in this way, "television news programs are extended advertizements for the structure of the society in which we live" (Edgar 1980:7).

A key feature of television news is its underlying "show biz" ethos and dominance by "entertainment values" (Postman 1985). Patricia Edgar (1980:1–2) argues that people do not want complicated newscasts; they want personalities, banter, comfort and assurance, cheap thrills, and amusement—in a word "entertainment."

As Dan Nimmo and James Combs (1985:8) note, "Entertainment rather than information values guide all TV programming, including news." This conclusion has led some analysts to apply labels like "minstrel show" and "circus" to television news broadcasts, "mixing show business with journalism" (Nimmo and Combs 1985:8). According to Neil Postman (1985:87–88), "A news show, to put it plainly, is a format for entertainment."

Not only is news entertainment but it also shares features with fictional genres. Park (quoted in Langer 1980:15) posits that "the news story and the fiction story are two forms of modern literature that are so alike one another that it is sometimes difficult to distinguish them." As Tuckman (quoted in Langer 1980:14) emphasizes, "reports of news events are stories—no more, no less," with features of "dramatic presentation," "rhetorical" devices, and narrative style that construct a "real-fictional world" out of the "newsworthy event" (Nimmo and Combs 1985:14–19). In other words, "television is a powerful fictional medium in contemporary society" (Brown 1990:17).

Finally, it is worth noting in passing Postman's (1985:8) view of the news as a "media event," a topographical feature of "a peek-a-boo world," where now this event, now that, pops into view for a moment, then vanishes again"; an "endless flow of bizarre juxtapositions" (Featherstone 1991:15). As summed up by Fisk (1989:181): "The news is a collage of fragmented images, and each image spawns more, calls up more, each image is a simulacrum—a perfect copy that has no original. The news is images of images of images—the final hyperreality" (see Eco 1987).

It is within these "readings" of the news as "anti-news," entertainment, fiction, and "hyperreality" that my visual material on serpent handling needs to be placed. The following examples of the representation of this religion on television reveal some of the conventional ways in which television has constructed and positioned these people; ways that share much with print and photojournalism as discussed before.

Terms such as "fragmented" and "disconnected" best characterize the first fleeting images of serpent handling which I am screening here. Although occurring in a documentary/educational frame rather than a news-magazine format, these brief but condensed images structure a reading of serpent handling as bizarre and detached from humanity.

The first quick flash of serpent handling comes from the *Faces of Culture* series in a half-hour program titled "Age and Common Interest" (SBS April 12, 1987). The fifteen seconds of serpent handling occur near the end of the program as part of a collage of disparate filmic images. David Carradine, the narrator, is discussing how anthropologists look at stratification and inequality by viewing these in a cultural context. He then mentions that the stratification of India, South Africa, and "America" may seem wrong, "just as some age grading may seem discriminating, and some common interest associations, frivolous or harmful," making the point that such groups serve functions in their respective societies.

The quick succession of images screened during this narration include a white doctor examining an underweight South African child, wealthy New Englanders opening frivolous but expensive Christmas presents, and a group of serpent handlers dancing about, holding snakes in the air, and shaking their heads, hands, and bodies to the spirited music. This is followed by the concluding scenes of the old Pullman porters from the film *Miles of Smiles, Years of Struggle*.

The inclusion of the serpent handling scenes seems gratuitous and arbitrary, for unlike the other footage used, "snake handling" was not depicted or discussed earlier in the program. It seemed free floating, discordant, and totally out of context. The narrator did not identify who these people are, where they live, what they are doing, or the meaning of it. They simply flashed onto the screen to be replaced by another set of images. But the old-timey clothes, style of music and singing, and obvious Anglo-Saxonness of the people give at least some signification that this is to be read as American South–Appalachia. In short, the overall effect strikes one as bizarre and literally meaningless behavior, reinforcing popular images of Holiness hill people.

The next two fragmentary reflections of serpent handling appear in a documentary, "Chase the Devil," that was presented on Australian television (SBS October 7, 1984) as part of a series with the unlikely title "Third World Music," unlikely because the film depicts contemporary music, religious and secular, in the southeastern United States, especially Nashville and parts of the Appalachian South.

Serpent handling is first shown near the beginning of the film. Fifty-five seconds of old black and white footage of part of a large Holiness revival presents images of serpent handling and very upbeat singing and dancing. It then focuses on three long-haired young girls wildly dancing a syncopated jitterbug to the accompaniment of guitars, tambourines, and clashing cymbals. They shake all over as in an epileptic fit, shaking their long hair about with abandon and ecstasy. The narrator explains: "Among the isolated settlers in the Appalachians, different religious sects evolved. The Holiness church, one extreme, praised the Lord with stringed instruments and even with the popular tunes of the day. They believed in the five signs of revelation, including serpent handling. At the other extreme were the primitive Baptists, many of whom believed music and dance to be the inspiration of the devil. Many thought that Holiness worshippers were little better than beasts." While the narration provides some locational and historical context, as before, the brief and fragmented nature of these frames do not establish the humanity of these objects of our gaze; rather they are positioned as other to and distant from us.

The second appearance of serpent handlers occurs in a two-minute-and-twelve-second segment that is an excerpt from a documentary film, *They Shall Take Up Serpents*, made in Carson Springs, Tennessee, in 1972. This clip depicts in very short sequence poison drinking, serpent handling, and an instance of serpent-bite, including a quick cut to the victim being prayed over in bed at the pastor's home. While still in church, the camera focuses on the victim, obviously in pain, who has slumped onto a church bench where people are frantically praying over him. The scene is one of pandemonium; his head falls back as he fights to retain consciousness and the bloodcurdling scream of a sister in the back of the small church house adds an eerie, grotesque, and shocking air to this heightened sequence.

I was present during the filming; in fact, I incidentally appear in it as the camera scans part of the congregation as the snakebite victim is helped out of church, and felt that the full twenty-minute "award-winning" documentary from which the snippets were extracted does not provide sufficient contextual and cultural information for a meaningful reading of this cultural scene. And appearing as it does in the "Third World Music" feature, it is almost totally meaningless, bizarre, and absurd.

The frequently screened promo for this program projected an even more decontextualized image of these people and their practices. I recall watching television in my living room in 1984 when, to my amazement, I saw on the screen my deceased Holiness friend, Jimmy Williams, in the space of a few seconds drink carbon tetrachloride, dance around, and handle serpents.

This documentary establishes the setting as "Appalachia" by giving a camera-eye view of passing in front of a long row of coal camp houses, people sitting on front porches, all to the accompaniment of "I'm Using My Bible for a Roadmap," sung by a banjo-strumming singer in a "Christian cafe." Interestingly, Carson Springs is not situated in a coal mining area but in the foothills of the Smoky Mountains; Appalachian to be sure, but not an accurate framing of these people who culturally are not the "typical" coal mining "snake handlers" of popular depiction.

The narrator introduces this scene by saying, "Some mountain folks' literal use of their Bibles as a roadmap has led them down unusual paths. Federal courts have tried to protect certain Holiness groups from the excesses of their own faith by outlawing their practices. In this privately taken film, worshippers proclaim their faith by drinking poison. To some, holding snakes is like touching the devil himself with all the excitement and tasting of forbidden fruit. One of the handlers has been bitten. This sect believes in the power of the Lord to heal. No medical help will be accepted. If he dies it is in the service of the Lord, fighting the devil."

I now turn to a news magazine "documentary" produced by the Australian Broadcasting Corporation (ABC) for the "7:30 Report" shown September 20, 1989, and screened again on April 29, 1990, as part of "Compass," a religious affairs program. The film runs for seven minutes and six seconds, plus short previews, which as discussed above present an even more fragmented, decontextualized image of the religion. This tightly constructed little film is a real genre piece and constructs mythical representations in every frame.

In announcing the segment on "snake handling" the host says, "And from the Appalachian Mountains, snakes add venom to religion." The establishing sequences show misty mountains and frame-by-frame shots of "Appalachian" scenes: houses, mobile homes, a man sitting on his front porch, "mountain" children pulling a wagon, a man in bibbed overalls lumbering past a house and walking away from the camera, and a close-up of a man's wrinkled face.

Each of these quick shots is in sync with the opening strums of "Duelling Banjos." The narration further establishes the context as "hillbillyland": "In these isolated valleys of the Appalachians there are no freeways, no jet airports, no five star hotels. The rugged hills keep the city slickers away. Here the kind name for the locals is mountain people; the unkind one is hillbillies. Many of them grind out a bare living in the coal mines. Life here may be tough, but these are people who believe that a better life lies beyond this one."

This film is fast paced with quick cuts and many close-ups of faces and people handling snakes. From the opening shots of "Appalachia," the film proceeds to a shot of the reporter standing in front of a country church with a forested mountain in the background and then changes to a preacher in the pulpit who speaks of snakes and the devil. The camera cuts to a group of women wearing granny dresses, standing with hands in the air, shifting from foot to foot. The narrator says, "They called this meeting their annual homecoming and some of the faithful drove eight hours to be here. They wore their Sunday best; they shook their tambourines. So, what's out of place here? Well for one thing those snakes in the boxes up on the platform." (Camera zooms in for close-up of snake rearing up in box.) "And why are there two bottles of poison sitting there?" (Close-up of two bottles labeled "poison" sitting in a basket.) "Come to mention it, that music owes more to Chuck Berry than it does to Charles Wesley." At this point the film shows musicians and singers along with members swaying and singing to the music. The narrator says: "They call themselves the Church of the Lord Jesus. To a thumping rock 'n roll beat they're working themselves up to a ritual of their church which they say is based on Saint Mark's Gospel. They're timber rattlers, a highly venomous local snake whose bite is often lethal. In the last forty years there have been eleven documented deaths by church members taking part in this ritual." The camera focuses on various people handling snakes and the narrator gives a brief historical sketch of serpent handling, mentioning that it is legal only in West Virginia, where this church is located.

The film then discovers that one of the handlers has been bitten some

Jim Birckhead 181

forty-seven times. After discussing this with the handler and showing frames of more snake handling, the narrator asserts that "wine is not the beverage of choice for communion in this church. Instead the pastor takes a healthy swig from a bottle which he says contains a mixture of strychnine and water and then passes it around. Either it contains a lot more water than strychnine or these people have very robust digestive systems." The film shows the pastor holding up the jar and then passing it to a man who drinks from it.

This is followed by more quick cuts of "snake handling" interspersed with a close-up of an extremely wrinkled-faced woman and other "mountain types." The closing collage focuses on a young brother's legs as he twirls about to the music and shows close-ups of snakes being handled. As this potpourri of images flashes past, the narrator concludes with the observation that "saving the faithful from death by snakebite may not be the most exalted task of the Deity, but for these folks it's tangible proof of His power. The only problem is that the fatality is equal proof of His power and is not particularly a pleasant way to go. Still, you've got to say that the music's got a great beat to it."

This piece is further framed as amusing, trivial, and hillbilly by the "7:30 Report" host: "Amazing! It's not Chuck Berry, though it's definitely Jerry Lee Lewis. In fact, Allen Hogan reckons that the local moonshine did him far more damage than the venom, and I can tell you that there's no truth in the rumor that out in the west of Queensland they're doing the same thing with taipans. That's it from us tonight, back tomorrow night after the news. Have a great day tomorrow. Good night" (theme music).

All in all, this short piece creates and reinforces popular views of Appalachian "otherness" and strangeness. Its ironic/humorous narration, opening banjo music, lack of depth, inaccuracies (for example, strychnine is not used as part of a communion service), close-up camera shots of "mountain" faces, quick cuts, shots of "good ole boys" in the background, emphasis on snakes and poison, lack of real context, and editing to bring out terse and humorous statements of church members all conspire to construct flattened, stock characters that are trotted out circus-style. We learn little of the context, theology, or meaning of these behaviors, or of the texture of these people's lives, hence of their humanity.

By trivializing in these ways, the economic, political, and social realities of these people's lives are obscured. It is ironic that the narrator speaks of isolation and "the rugged hills" that "keep the city slickers away" as this coal mining area of West Virginia has long been controlled by outside multinational mining corporations and these people's lives affected by the boom-and-bust cycles of the world coal market. The text gives itself away in two places; first, by mentioning how the people "grind out a bare living in the coal mines" and, second, when it notes that "some of the faithful drove eight hours to be here." But it fails to make the connection between these two observations or develop the implications of this for our understanding of this religion in context. Namely, because of high unemployment, people from such communities have had to leave the region to find work. Consequently, the church featured here at Mico, West Virginia, is part of a loose confederation of two other churches presided over by a bishop in Columbus, Ohio (not mentioned in the film). There is considerable visiting back and forth between the Columbus, Kistler, and Mico churches, much of which relates to out-migration, hence the reason why some people have driven so far for the "homecoming," undermining the film's premise of pristine mountain isolation.

As I mentioned before, this short news magazine feature was screened again in 1990 as part of a serious religious affairs digest. Even in this context, the host's framing unintentionally revealed the working of stereotype. In introducing the film, she states that "small communities cut off from the mainstream have been known to develop strange beliefs and rituals. One such group is the fundamentalist, hillbilly Church of the Lord Jesus in the Appalachian Mountains of America." The association of serpent handlers with "hillbilly" seems to be ingrained and inevitable.

Programs like this that strive for high standards of objectivity and respect for various religious traditions seem to lapse when it comes to a religion such as Holiness serpent handling. The same series, for example, screened an excellent documentary on serpent handling in 1988. The final program of the year concluded with a collage of the humorous moments of the year; a serious remark made by a Holiness preacher about the "two kinds of people who would handle a snake" naturally was included, not to mention the sensationalistic promos to advertise the original program.

The second "documentary" we look at was produced by the BBC

in 1983, and *The Listener* magazine cover story (Esler 1983) featured aspects of its making. Although more substantial (seventeen minutes and forty-five seconds), serious, and less sensationalistic than the Australian film, the BBC film nonetheless constructs and perpetuates standard Appalachian stereotypes of "otherness" and "hillbilliness." I will review only the main features of this production, which was shown in BBC2's "Newsnight" program in the United Kingdom (tape courtesy of the Reverend Alfred Ball).

The film begins with the obligatory mountainscapes, shots of rural "folk" in bibbed overalls, and the background sound of banjo chords. We are told by the narrator, in effect, that these people live in archaic time in "the southern Bible Belt" where "religion like so much else is homespun." He establishes the context by sketching this picture: "Sunrise over the Smoky Mountains of east Tennessee, one of the most beautiful areas of America's old South, where Jefferson and Cocke counties meet the foothills of the Smokies in an area of tobacco, corn, and stock farmers, independent and often poor families who sometimes don't take too kindly to strangers. It's a remote reminder of America as it used to be, where if you couldn't grow it you couldn't have it and where they still maintain strong conservative traditions; close to nature, close to the soil, and close to God."

The opening sketch, although picturesque, is not an accurate reflection of the Holiness people being portrayed here. The local color visuals of standard mountain types were not of people in this church, few of whom are farmers. Situated as it is near Newport and close to Gatlinburg and Pigeon Forge, this church tends to attract people who work in the many manufacturing plants in the area, drive trucks, or work in the local tourist and hospitality industry.

The myth-making of the film is supported further by the *Listener* article, which, like the film, emphasizes local color and "down home" images. The pastor, for example, is said to be a lumberjack; he is, in fact, a tree surgeon and at the time of the filming was a partner in a business that repaired video games and installed satellite space dishes. Similarly, the photo of "snake handling" used in the article is a file photo and not of the people being written about.

Near the conclusion of the film the narrator constructs the fiction of serpent handlers' secretiveness. Because serpents were not taken up during the service that they filmed, it was concluded that "it seemed as if because God had not anointed Alfred, or because at the last minute he, like the others, wished to keep their secrets that outsiders would not see the much heralded taking up of serpents. He decreed shortly before eleven o'clock that it would not happen." In fact, the reason the pastor did not handle serpents was not because "he wished to keep their secrets" (an absurd suggestion considering the previously discussed media coverage of serpent handling in this area) but that this church had all but discontinued the practice and had even informed the BBC reporter that serpent handling would probably not occur.

The narrator then reports: "But as members of the church slowly drifted out it became clear that if the shepherd was not anointed to handle poisonous snakes, part of his flock was." The film then depicts a brother handling a snake and testifying outside the church. This handler was not part of the "flock" as alleged in the film but a media hungry "saint" from a rival congregation. This is a reflection of the un-"ethnographicness" (Heider 1976:3) of such films, as no account is given of the process used in selecting interviewees or how such people represent or do not represent the reality being portrayed. Similarly, people who make such films rarely spend more than a few days or a week at most in the community. The BBC crew, I was told by church members, spent about a week in east Tennessee mostly driving around the countryside shooting various takes of rural Appalachian context, but spent relatively little time with church members.

Other news "documentaries" that I have seen about this religion use similar devices to create similar fictional clichés of essential bizarreness and "otherness," largely in the name of human interest and entertainment. These, along with print media features on serpent handling, feed into and form part of larger discourses that serve to construct these people as a metaphor of "Appalachia," which, as Newcomb (1979–80:55) argues, is "a metaphor of the South as a whole."

WILL THE CIRCLE BE UNBROKEN?

I will not attempt to fill this discursive space (see Rose 1991) with additional interpretation or summarizing of my observations and arguments; these points have been made throughout the paper. Rather, I will allow a medley of recent "voices" to evoke and to encapsulate the concluding resonances of my paper, once again pointing to questions of representation, availability of images of serpent handling, media genre conventions, superficiality and trivialization of stories, and bias, in short, the popular media construction of a southern stereotype.

The first voice is that of the Reverend Alfred Ball animatedly delivering the message at a Wednesday night church service (April 17, 1991) at the Full Gospel Tabernacle near Cosby, Tennessee, the setting of a number of media pieces on Holiness religion (although serpent handling is no longer practiced there).[5] "There is a hillbilly stereotype. They say we're ignorant, barefoot, illiterate, uneducated, unshaven, wearing only overalls with nothing on underneath, only been to the local town once or twice and got lost then. The image is that only hillbillies are Christians and love God."

The second voice is journalistic, part of a wire service story published in our local newspaper, *The Border Mail*, July 17, 1991, under the headline "Once Bitten . . .":

> New York, Tues: A man whose stepfather appealed a State ban on snake handling in the U.S. Supreme Court has died from a snakebite. Jimmy Ray Williams was bitten on the right arm by a 90cm black timber rattler on Saturday during a service at the House of Prayer in Jesus's Name. In 1974, Williams's stepfather Pastor Liston Pack appealed Tennessee's snake handling ban to the U.S. Supreme Court, but lost. Williams's father, Jimmy Ray Williams Sr., died in 1973 after drinking strychnine during a service. Some small religious sects in the U.S. use snake handling as part of their worship service.

The third voice is televisual-documentary, a forty-three-second snippet on Holiness serpent handling included in a wildlife program shown on the Australian ABC, "A Most Remarkable Planet" ("Fear of the Wild"): "Tonight, some animals are worshipped as Gods, others ridiculed as clowns" (*The Border Mail*, October 13, 1991). Sandwiched between scenes from a Texas rattlesnake round-up that graphically depicts a number of snakes being chopped in half by a large machete ("The only good rattlesnake is a dead one") and the Italian celebration of the Feast of Saint Dominic, these fleeting seconds capture the full "snake handling boogie" of a group of handlers, snakes held high, ecstatically dancing about on a raised platform to pounding gospel rock music. The voice-over explains: "More than other animals snakes are traditional symbols of evil. In the Bible Satan himself is represented by one, and in parts of the Appalachian Mountains, the faithful challenge Satan in a literal response to Saint Mark's instructions: 'They shall take up serpents.' Handlers of rattlers and cottonmouths submit themselves utterly to God's will. True believers will survive a bite."

The final voice is the sensationalistic tabloid coverage of the July 17 snakebite death noted above but not appearing until October 1, 1991, on p. 31 of *The National Examiner*.[6] The headline "Rattlesnake Kills Man During Church Service" flows from a sketch of the open jaws of a rattlesnake. "It held on to his wrist and wouldn't let go" appears in large white print next to a photo of a man, mouth open, arms raised, hands thrust out, holding two snakes tangled around one another with the caption: "Deadly Act: Jimmy Ray Williams Jr. met the same fate as religious snake handler Charles Prince (above), who died in 1985" and above a photo of "Lawmen Charles Long and Larry Samsel inspect[ing] the House of Prayer." The story begins in bold print with: "Churchgoer Jimmy Ray Williams Jr. tested his fearless faith in two biblical passages against the deadly bite of a 3-foot rattlesnake—and lost." It continues:

> Within two hours, the 28-year old from Hot Springs, North Carolina was dead. But his host minister, charismatic Pastor Marvin "Bud" Gregg of the snake-handling, strychnine-swigging House of Prayer in Jesus' Name church outside Morristown, Tennessee, assured 200 mourners: "If we ever see Jimmy Ray again, we'll see a crown of righteousness on his head." . . . Believers put their faith in divine protection through Mark 16:18 and Luke 10:19, which say true believers can't be harmed by poisonous serpents, scorpions or drinks. . . .
>
> Hamblen Country Detective Larry Samsel told *The Examiner*: "This is pretty shocking stuff to most of us. But it's hard to put a case together without witnesses unless an officer was present during the snake-biting." Pastor Gregg told investigators: "I was handling the serpents with other members that Saturday evening, and looked over and saw Jimmy Ray was, too. At 8:20 I saw a black timber rattler bite him on his wrist. It held on and Jimmy Ray pulled it four times before jerking it loose and putting it in a box.
>
> "His brother, Allen, came to pray for Jimmy Ray and asked if he wanted to go to a doctor. Jimmy Ray refused but said he felt numb all over. Shortly after that he got sick."
>
> Williams was taken to a parishioner's home. There, cops and paramedics were called in, but they were too late to revive him. Williams was rushed to the hospital, where he was pronounced dead on arrival.

Later, Allen Williams dismissed his brother's dramatic demise as merely "an incident between him and the Lord."

NOTES

1. I use "snake handler" in a marked sense throughout this paper, as the Tennessee people with whom I worked saw themselves as serpent handlers or Holiness people. As my friend of the past twenty years, the Reverend Alfred Ball, was fond of saying, "Snake handlers are in the circus."
2. I quote these excerpts from this play with the kind permission of Alexander Speer of the Actors Theatre of Louisville, trustee for Jane Martin.
3. This title is taken from chapter 1 of John F. Day's *Bloody Ground* (1941). "Mountain Voodoo" in its "shocked reportage" (Shapiro 1983:163) of "snake handling" exemplifies the genre of chapter-length journalistic-fictional descriptions of this faith.
4. In exploring this with students it appears that their "reading" of the documentary draws on a wealth of stereotyped background meanings about "hillbillies" as humorous, ridiculous, or bizarre derived from such sources as *Li'l Abner*, *The Beverly Hillbillies*, *Deliverance*, and any number of feature films about the South.
5. Interestingly, after this service Al and I discussed my paper and the script of the play *Holy Ghosts* (Linney 1971) sent to him by a theater director in Dallas, Texas, as well as a short story by Fee (1989), "The Night I Lost My Religion at the 'Holy Roller' Church."
6. I thank Jackie (Sexton) Ward, former Caney Creek, Kentucky, resident, now of Vancouver, British Columbia, for sending me this article about the snakebite death of my first "informant's" son.

REFERENCES

ALTHER, LISA, 1977. *Kinflicks* (New York: Penguin).
BAKHTIN, MIKHAIL, 1981. *The Dialogic Imagination* (Austin: University of Texas Press).
BERGER, JOHN, 1972. *Ways of Seeing* (London: British Broadcasting Corporation/Penguin).
BRANSCOME, JAMES, 1971. Annihilating the Hillbilly: The Appalachians' Struggle with America's Institutions. *Katallagete* (Winter): 25–42.

BROWN, MARY ELLEN, 1990. Introduction: Feminist Cultural Television Criticism—Culture, Theory and Practice. In *Television And Women's Culture—The Politics of the Popular*, Mary Ellen Brown, ed. (Sydney: Currency Press), pp. 11–22.

Chase the Devil, 1984. Film. Third World Music. Special Broadcasting Service (SBS). October 7.

CLARK, DANAE, 1990. Cagney and Lacey: Feminist Strategies of Detection. In *Television and Women's Culture—The Politics of the Popular*, Mary Ellen Brown, ed. (Sydney: Currency Press), pp. 117–33.

CLEMENTS, WILLIAM H., 1977. Review Essay: Snake-handlers on Film. *Journal of American Folklore* 90:502–6.

——— 1979. Film Review, "The Jolo Serpent-Handlers." *Journal of American Folklore* 92:127–28.

CONNELL, R. W., 1977. *Ruling Class, Ruling Culture* (Cambridge: Cambridge University Press).

DARNELL, REGNA, 1991. Ethnographic Genre and Poetic Voice. In *Anthropological Poetics*, Ivan Brady, ed. (Savage, Md.: Rowman and Littlefield), pp. 267–77.

DAY, JOHN F., 1941. *Bloody Ground* (New York: Doubleday Doran and Co.).

DRUMMOND, LEE, 1983. Jonestown: A Study in Ethnographic Discourse. *Semiotica* 46:167–209.

ECO, UMBERTO, 1987. *Travels in Hyperreality* (London: Pan Books).

EDGAR, PATRICIA, 1980. Introduction. In *The News In Focus: The Journalism of Exception*, Patricia Edgar, ed. (Melbourne: Macmillan Company of Australia), pp. 1–12.

ESLER, GAVIN, 1983. Snakes in Church. *The Listener*. August 18:2–4.

FEATHERSTONE, MIKE, 1991. *Consumer Culture & Postmodernism* (London: Sage).

FEE, JERRY R., 1989. The Night I Lost My Religion at the "Holy Roller" Church. *Appalachian Heritage* 17:41–47.

FISK, JOHN, 1989. *Reading The Popular* (Boston: Unwin Hyman).

FORTUNATO, FRANK, 1980. Snake Handlers: Risking Death as a Test of Faith. *Hustler* 6:50–58; 123–24.

GOSSETT, LOUISE Y., 1965. *Violence in Recent Southern Fiction* (Durham: Duke University Press).

HEIDER, KARL G. 1976. *Ethnographic Film* (Austin: University of Texas Press).

LANGER, JOHN, 1980. The Structure and Ideology of the "Other News" on Television. In *The News In Focus: The Journalism of Exception*. Patricia Edgar, ed. (Melbourne: The Macmillan Company of Australia), pp. 13–43.

LINNEY, ROMULUS, 1971. *Holy Ghosts* (New York: Dramatists Play Service).

MCNEIL, WILLIAM K., 1977. Appalachian Folklore Scholarship. *Appalachian Journal* 5:55–64.
———, ed., 1989. *Appalachian Images in Folk and Popular Culture* (Ann Arbor: UMI Research Press).
MAGGARD, SALLY WARD, 1983–84. Cultural Hegemony: The News Media and Appalachia. *Appalachian Journal* 11:67–83.
MARTIN, JANE, 1983. *Talking With . . .* (New York: Samuel French).
MAURER, B. B., 1978. Introduction. In *Religion in Appalachia*, John D. Photiadis, ed. (Morgantown: University of West Virginia Press), pp. 1–5.
NEWCOMB, HORACE, 1979–80. Appalachia on Television: Region as Symbol in American Popular Culture. *Appalachian Journal* 7:155–64.
NIMMO, DAN, and JAMES E. COMBS, 1985. *Nightly Horrors: Crisis Coverage in Television Network News* (Knoxville: University of Tennessee Press).
POSTMAN, NEIL, 1985. *Amusing Ourselves to Death: Public Discourse in the Age of Show Business* (London: Heinemann).
RITCHIN, FRED, 1990. *In Our Own Image: The Coming Revolution in Photography* (New York: Aperture).
ROSE, DAN, 1991. Reversal. In *Anthropological Poetics*, Ivan Brady, ed. (Savage, Md.: Rowman and Littlefield), pp. 283–301.
SELTZER, CURTIS, 1978. The Media vs. Appalachia: A Case Study. In *Teaching Mountain Children*, David N. Mielke, ed. (Boone, N.C.: Appalachian Consortium Press), pp. 130–34.
SHAPIRO, HENRY D., 1983. John F. Day and the Disappearance of Appalachia from the American Consciousness. *Appalachian Journal* 10:157–64.
TINDALL, GEORGE B., 1989. Mythic South. In Wilson and Ferris, eds., *Encyclopedia of Southern Culture*, pp. 1097–99.
WHISNANT, DAVID E., 1979–80. Introduction, Special Cultural Issue. *Appalachian Journal* 7:5–8.
WILSON, CHARLES REAGAN, and WILLIAM FERRIS, eds., 1989. *Encyclopedia of Southern Culture* (Chapel Hill: University of North Carolina Press).

The Worm and the Snake
Benjamin Dunlap

Columbia, S. C.

On my way to meet Stan, I hear on the news that a plane has crashed at Tan Son Nhut. Two hundred children are dead. The newscaster says they were refugees, among the last to get out.

I'm the first to arrive, so I wait on the porch, watching early spring besplatter the government compound. Past a whitewashed wall is the governor's mansion. To the left of that is the Baptist Center, then the columned facade of New South Life. The shadows are blue on the gray flagstones.

This building was once a private home, its wrought-iron work, like a dowager's shawl, evoking what our leaders call "the southern way of life," though for them, after dark, in this old part of town, it's probably closer to Saigon—the streets belong to the people they fear. In the morning they shift their talk again to winning the hearts and minds, which is how I first meet Stan.

I write book reviews for *The New Republic*. That doesn't cut ice with Stan, of course, but I also teach a movie course at the local university. I've just finished class when he gives me a call. We've never met, but he wants to know if I'll help introduce a film.

I ask him where.

"John's Island," he says. "A black community center."

Gullah country, I think—though, since they got lucky at Hilton Head, developers are in a frenzy. I hear the coast is like Cam Ran Bay. I ought to see it before it goes.

"I'll send you a print. Gretchen Robinson's film *The People Who Take Up Serpents*."

"Snake handling, huh?"

It's just a guess. As far as I know that appeals to blacks about as much as "Hee Haw."

"We're building bridges."

"From Greenville," he adds. "And east Tennessee. Down to the Gullah coast."

"The worm and the snake."

"Right on!" he laughs, as if he thinks I've made a witty comment.

What I'm thinking about is Hollings's report to the Senate Select Committee. Ascaris worms are rife on the coast. A doctor named Gatch got a lot of press for trying to help the blacks. His neighbors talked him into leaving.

"The worm and the snake," Stan laughs again. "That's pretty good. You know you'll have a confederate."

"A what?" I ask.

"His name is Bone. He's an anthropologist."

This is all I know before we leave, although I screen the film. It's hard to imagine bridges from that. Poverty pocket to poverty pocket.

I'm still on the porch when I see Doctor Bone. He's as courtly as a Watusi prince, with puffs of hair over either ear, a gray moustache, and an amulet. The amulet seems to be made of bone, with fur and leather trimmings. His accent's very elegant—from Guyana, he tells me when I ask. He's teaching at South Carolina State.

We hear a honk from a black sedan. The driver is in a safari shirt with epaulets and loops for shells. Also granny glasses and Fab Four hair.

"Have you met Stan?" asks Doctor Bone, who likes to take control.

That's evident at the interstate, when he spots a joint with a Miller's sign. It is concrete block, with rooms in back and doors that are painted pistachio.

"Good place for coffee," he observes.

I'd like to look for another place, but he takes umbrage and Stan pulls in. Stan doesn't get out while we go in, past a door decal ("SAILORS HAVE MORE FUN") and some sort of puddle on the floor. It's dank and gloomy—a counter and a couple of stools.

But something approaches across the dance floor. Hip-huggers and a halter top. A teeny-bopper in a wig. She looks like Little Orphan Annie, except she's more pneumatic.

"Three coffees to go," says Doctor Bone in a voice like Nat King Cole.

The girl doesn't move. Two goons slouch in. They're sipping Buds for breakfast. Doctor Bone looks slowly from side to side like some sort of wading bird.

"Also," he says, "one order of toast."

The girl has moved up close to him and is staring at his amulet. The larger goon's head is trapezoidal, narrowing sharply toward the crown. The other has ham-hock arms that dangle. He's staring hard at Doctor Bone.

"No toast," says the trapezoidal goon, but Doctor Bone ignores him.

"Muffins, if you have them."

I see the goon is about to reply and I improvise a manic spiel, in the midst of which we get three cups. Annie holds two fingers up as she puts the cups down on the counter. Without asking what the fingers mean, I leave two dollars and move toward the door, still talking fast, not looking back.

"Hey!" says a goon, but we get in the car and hit the interstate.

Doctor Bone's amused.

"Did I pass?" he asks.

"You escaped," I tell him.

We stop for lunch on the outskirts of Charleston, at a place called Long John Silver's. It's a new franchise with a boat dock façade and waitresses dressed in jolly rogers. Everything's on a doll's house scale, including the plaster tidbit shrimp like "The Tale of Two Bad Mice."

John's Island is only a mile away. The community center turns out to be the local Mt. Zion church, which offers another parallel: two poor white churches in the highlands, a poor black church on the coast.

"There's something else," Stan looks around. "The audience might be kind of old."

I've prepared a psychedelic speech, which I start to revise in my mind.

"Some might be deaf. One or two are blind. It's a senior citizen's center."

Before I can speak he changes the subject.

"Looks like Gretchen's here already."

This is also news. He hadn't told us she'd be coming.

"Why doesn't Gretchen introduce it?"

"She's shy," Stan says. "It was her first film. Besides, you know, she got pretty involved. She'd been working as a journalist."

I ask him what she's doing here.

"She's making a film about Gullah."

Oho, I think. It's clearer now. We're here as Gretchen's endorsements. My problem is I don't like the film. I'm mulling this over as we enter a building beside the church. On one side is a cemetery, with Spanish moss and a couple of wreaths, red, white, and blue in the undergrowth.

On the other side is a long, low hut, emitting a sort of murmur.

"We're a little late." Stan looks at his watch. "You've screened it already, right?"

I nod as my eyes adjust to the dark. He gestures towards a compact brunette who's tending the projector. We're introduced in a whispery way, after which she moves to adjust a knob and we stumble towards some folding chairs. Doctor Bone's baritone causes heads to turn. Eight heads in all, not including a woman in red-rimmed glasses who's standing by the door. She looks official. The rest are old, their faces so dark their features vanish. Only two are men. One with his hands folded over a cane is staring at me with rheumy eyes. Maybe he can't see the screen. The room's too light and the sound's distorted.

I ask for directions to the toilet. Long John has got me in his grip. On my way down the hall, I pass a room of children with their heads on their desks. They seem to be listening to the film, which has got to sound bizarre to them: voices of crackers testifying, inviting us to see their snakes, explaining listlessly as they rock how much their faith has meant to them. A reason for living is how they put it. Christ calls the poor in worldly goods who're rich in the things of the spirit.

Whatever they hear, the children can't see the littered ravines or the church that looks like a roadside shack, plunked down across from some modern buildings. Maybe they hear the electric guitars and the sound of tires crunching gravel. But how can they guess at the station wagons, the buckets of Kentucky Fried, the fluorescent Last Supper on the wall? They don't get to see how the faithful move: the snap-and-flap of a marionette, the ponderous gesticulation, embracing like soldiers before a battle. They hear a gibber of unknown tongues, but the accent must sound even stranger. The snakes, of course, make no sound at all. The faithful hold them in writhing bunches—bucking with galvanic spasms, not dancing but convulsing.

One of the children is peering at me, as if he thought I was part of the show. I flash a "V" and go down the hall. As I enter the room a voice from the screen denies that they're testing their faith at all. They're trying to confirm the gospel. He's alluding to that passage in Mark when the risen Christ makes promises: "These signs shall follow them that believe; In my name shall they cast out devils; They shall speak with new tongues; They shall take up serpents; And if they drink any deadly thing, it shall not hurt them."

If that's not right, a snake handler says, "then none of the rest of hit's right." One of them demonstrates a flame that doesn't burn the flesh. It also fails to singe their sleeves—but it's clear to me their conviction is real. They identify with the early Christians, who were also hounded by the law. They hold no truck with conventional faith (it's "dry as a soda cracker," they say, and "dead as a doornail" too).

They have their own proprieties. The women sit apart from the men (they might not know what to make of Freud, but they know what happened in the garden). They haven't seen Georgina Spelvin, but they know the serpent is after sex. It's the Devil, they say, who tempted Eve . . . which is why their women don't wear cosmetics, or curl their hair, or drink Coca-Cola. Strychnine's sometimes in a service, but medicine shows lack of faith. No whiskey, no sex, no drugs they say. ("We're holy," I hear, "but we don't roll.") It's the serpent whose motion is sinuous, the faithful lurch and twitch and jerk. If Freudians think the snake is phallic, their ecstasy doesn't look erotic—it's more like a junkie shooting up. (Mainlining the Word, I think to myself. That rush of danger is their fix, embracing what they ought to flee, so that fear itself short-circuits the brain, producing a high like heroin.) As old as Adam and older than Eve.

I look again at our audience, who seem so inert and inscrutable. The ancient worm is not in their hands, but it's probably in their bellies. The senator's vowed to abolish it, as the sheriff says he'd get rid of the snakes—as Westmoreland swears he'll kill VC. But such parallels don't help me much. Nobody's asking for parasites. The faithful want to pick up snakes, and the Viet Cong are shooting back. The constant is extermination . . . that and their origins in the sticks. But cruising the sticks takes a lot of mileage, and the preachers for these snake-handling cults are constantly on the move, like circuit riders I'd almost say, except their angular movement style reflects the machines that nurtured them: the textile mill and the automobile.

Snake handling began in 1909, in Grasshopper Valley, Tennessee. A man named Hensley read Saint Mark and decided he ought to check it out. At seventy a rattler got him, after forty-six years of handling snakes in an ever narrowing circle. It occurs to me that sea island blacks must move to other rhythms. When *they* light out it's straight line shots, to Michigan or Philadelphia. Only the old and the young remain . . . and those beneath the moss outside, whom the alien worm possesses forever. The poor whites migrated to the mills. Their scourge was pellagra and malnutrition. The Gullah blacks are being invaded—by tourists and developers. Their scourge is ascaris and malnutrition. What they have in common isn't just faith. It's neglect and exploitation.

The movie ends, but nobody stirs. Doctor Bone makes a gesture for me to go first while Gretchen is still rewinding the film.

"I'm an English professor," is how I start.

They give me the sceptical courtesy they'd give a white gang boss. But I'm eager to build Stan's bridge for him. I'm full of the age-old liberal dream of uniting the dispossessed.

"Those people you saw are victims," I say. "Of poverty and neglect."

They look comatose. I broaden my gestures just a bit. Gretchen is watching with a frown.

"It's right to admire their dedication. It's right to ask why other churches have proved so inadequate. But it's wrong to accept the poverty from which their faith derives."

It's clear to me I'm not getting through. I back up and start again.

"The Bible says 'these signs shall follow them that believe . . .' "

I quote Saint Mark to no avail. Maybe I need to speak in Gullah.

"Snake handling is a modern invention. It's not a tradition from the past. It grows out of poverty and neglect."

I'm repeating myself, but what can I do? I'm as much an outsider as the sheriff.

"Most of those people," I declaim, "are hardly able to read and write."

How dumb can you get? Their faces are blank. I cast about for another handle.

"Remember how Satan tempted Christ?"

Now there's a movement to my right. A birdlike woman has nodded her head, but it's possible she's just waking up.

"He asked him to prove that he was God."

She nods again and makes a noise. She definitely agrees with me.

"What if I called on Satan now?"

They're riveted.

"What if I'd brought a box of snakes and said . . ."

I make a dramatic gesture.

"I'll do what Jesus wouldn't do! I'll . . ."

Suddenly there's a fruit-basket turnover. The birdlike woman emits a shriek. The old man with the yellow eyes is waving his cane about.

"It shall bruise thy heel!" he says with a whoop as the woman in glasses heads his way.

"AND THOU SHALT BRUISE HIS HEAD!"

He thumps the floor, but she grabs the cane, helping the bird woman back to her chair.

"There's no snakes here!" she says severely.

"No snakes!" I echo.

But nobody hears until Moses' voice booms over the din.

"People! People!"

It's Doctor Bone, quelling the panic in a flash.

"My colleague has spoken," he begins.

They seem to think he's a black-skinned martian.

"I'd like to know," he coaxes them, "should somebody tell you how to worship?"

"Huh-uh! No, suh!" the voices erupt.

"Those people you watched with rattlesnakes see God in their own way. Do you want them put in jail for that?"

"Huh-uh! No way!"

The woman in glasses raises her hand.

"They've got a right to practice their faith, but not to hurt other people."

The audience nod while Doctor Bone pauses, apparently deep in meditation. He looks at everyone in turn.

"Has anyone here ever felt the spirit?"

A hesitation. Then a huge-bosomed woman sighs and says, "The spirit's moved me many times."

She beams as if she's testifying.

"I used to belong to a Holiness church."

She says they didn't handle snakes, but they often washed each other's feet. She's a Methodist now, though she sometimes misses the Holiness fellowship.

"They be better Christians," she remembers.

Doctor Bone looks over at me.

"I'd like to leave you with one thought."

I see Gretchen is smiling with satisfaction.

"Judge not," he says, "that ye be not judged."

"Tha's right!" they answer. "Uh-huh! Tha's right!"

I'm mortified, with no rejoinder. But the yellow-eyed man is back on his feet.

"I would not that ye be *ignorant!*"

The voice is husky but defiant. Now it's Doctor Bone who's disconcerted.

"Neither let us tempt *Christ,*" says yellow-eyes, "as some of *them* were also tempted . . ."

Doctor Bone can't hold this floodtide back.

". . . and were destroyed by SERPENTS!"

"Sweet Jesus!" croons a woman in blue.

"Thou shalt have no other gods but ME!"

The woman in glasses signals to Stan.

"Ahhh-MEN!"

The old man gropes for his cane, and with that our meeting's over. The chagrin I feel is mixed with relief. I haven't passed, but I think I've escaped. Outside the door, the birdlike woman comes up to shake my hand.

"Glad you could come!" she says over and over. "Hope you can come again."

The woman in glasses leads her away. The yellow-eyed man is waiting his turn. He seems to think Doctor Bone is my uncle and wants us to know that his great-granddaughter is in college in New Jersey. He used to be a preacher, he says. The woman in glasses calls him inside.

"Now we get our lunch," the old man smiles.

I glance at my watch. It's after three.

We drive several miles to Angel Oak, a majestic tree that's threatened by progress. A couple of teenage blacks are there, laughing and holding hands. They drive away when they see us. The four of us walk around the tree, appraising its antiquity. Its limbs twist outward from its trunk like a spiral nebula. Empty fields in all directions. Gretchen corners me by the fence.

"Stan says you went to Harvard."

I know from her tone what she's getting at.

"For graduate school. Before that I was in east Tennessee. I knew people like the ones in your film."

"I doubt it," she says. "You wouldn't be so condescending."

"Excuse me," Doctor Bone jumps in. "I think it's a matter of not conceding what happens in a ritual. In Africa and the Middle East the snake is a very ancient symbol. It mediates between two worlds."

"That's irrelevant," I say to him. "Those people don't have a past or future. What they do with snakes is as far from Jung as that tacky painting is from Da Vinci."

"You remind me," he says, "of an ancient Roman . . ."

His voice is calm, but I see he's annoyed.

". . . denouncing the Christians for being vulgar."

Gretchen smirks. I find I'm nettled.

"It's not vulgarity," I say. "It's poverty that produces such mutations. Such morbid blooms. Like hothouse orchids, rooted in nothing at all."

Gretchen squares off. Her head is lowered.

"You think I'm too objective."

This puzzles me and I don't reply.

"You're like Grierson. You want polemic."

"I didn't say that. I think you show what you think you saw. But I also think you're omitting a lot."

"Like what?" she asks.

"Dissension," I say.

"I show what happened when I was there."

"Well, what about blacks? You say that sometimes they attend, but we never see them once in the film. And I've heard about that rift they had when a woman said . . ."

"How'd you know about that?"

"What sort of rift," asks Doctor Bone.

"She wanted to be a minister. But that didn't happen while I was there."

"My point is that it wouldn't have happened if you had never been there."

"She's not ethnographic? Is that your point?"

"He's trying to get us off the point."

"It's ethnographic," I tell them both. "But the images contradict the words. What really strikes me is the clutter, a faith that's been jerry-built up there from the Appalachian junkyard. All those busted appliances on the porches, those bed springs rusting in the gully. Whatever they say, what the pictures show is a poor, white cargo cult. Not our antithesis at all—our lowest common denominator."

"And you'd do what?" asks Doctor Bone. "Give them money so they can shop first class? Invite them to a uptown church?"

For the first time since I saw this film, I know what I really want to say.

"You have these people," I insist. "Uprooted, exploited, and despised. All they really know is anxiety, insecurity, and fear. That's what they're so busy ritualizing. It's not the Devil they take up, except inasmuch as they suppose he's the instrument of their trouble. It's not even sex, except inasmuch as that's among the things forbidden—forbidden by God, forbidden by law, forbidden by their situation. And nothing confirms their view of the world so much as persecution. That's what they really triumph over. But in fact they get no more control than they've ever managed to have—only a brief deluded escape, for which they're willing to risk their lives. Is telling them to go ahead the best you can do for them?"

"Instead of what?" asks Doctor Bone.

"I don't know," I say. "Unionizing the mills. Enforcing the school attendance laws. Improving social services maybe."

"And what if they'd rather handle snakes?"

I shrug. I haven't thought this far.

"Television," I say. "The global village. We'll help them develop a new perspective."

Gretchen emits a short, harsh laugh.

"I guess you'd want the same things here?"

John's Island, she means.

"They have more to lose."

"More what?" she asks.

I want to say at least they have a past.

"Weren't *they* uprooted?" Gretchen asks. "You think their culture's so pathetic?"

She knows I don't. It's rhythmic, graceful, sinuous. But I suddenly see how southern poor whites have always been the odd man out and I feel ashamed of my prejudice.

"What I'd like to know," says Doctor Bone, who's back in his Moses mode again, "since you think those people are aberrant. You know, of course, that to most outsiders the South itself is an aberration?"

I nod, but I don't try to answer.

"As a matter of fact, to most outsiders the United States is an aberration. So explain to me, as a non-American, what's been going on in Vietnam? Is handling snakes less civilized? More violent? Less rational?"

"I'm opposed to both," I start to say, but Stan interrupts us at this point.

"We've got to get back."

I shrug as Doctor Bone nods and smiles. He's a jerk, I think, though I can't decide where my cleverness went wrong. We drop Gretchen off and drive back home in our air-conditioned car.

On the way we pass a roadside cross with the single word "PREPARE." But we talk about innocuous things—whether people who lead such lives as ours have the time to bring up children. It's dark when we get home.

NOTE

The People Who Take Up Serpents, by Gretchen Robinson, can be rented for nonprofit use in South Carolina from the South Carolina Arts Commission, 1800 Gervais St., Columbia, S.C. 29201. The format is 16mm and the fee is $25.

Contributors

ALEX ALBRIGHT is an assistant professor of nonfiction writing in the English department, East Carolina University. His writings about *Pitch a Boogie Woogie* and related research interests have appeared in *American Film*, the Center for Black Music Research *Bulletin*, *Living Blues*, and other regional publications. He wrote and produced the UNC-TV documentary *Boogie in Black and White*, which includes the complete "Pitch a Boogie Woogie" and has been shown on PBS affiliates in thirty-two states. He is director of the North Carolina Film Project and editor of the *North Carolina Literary Review*.

JIM BIRCKHEAD is a senior lecturer in anthropology and Aboriginal studies and member of the Johnstone Centre of Parks, Recreation and Heritage at Charles Sturt University, Albury, N.S.W., Australia. He received his Ph.D. from the University of Alberta in 1976 and formerly taught at Tennessee Technological University. His research interests include questions of cultural representation, popular media and minority group identity, and the cultural politics of "tradition" with respect to "Appalachia" and Aboriginal Australia. He has conducted ethnographic research in Australia and in various communities in the southern Appalachians intermittently since 1965.

BENJAMIN DUNLAP received his Ph.D. in English literature from Harvard. He is Chapman Professor of Humanities at Wofford College. He has written and produced many dramas, documentaries, and performing arts programs for PBS and the South Carolina ETV Network.

ROBERT GIPE works for Appalshop, a media arts and education center in Whitesburg, Kentucky.

KARL G. HEIDER is a professor of anthropology at the University of South Carolina. His main current research is on emotions in Indonesia (especially the Minangkabau of Sumatra). He has made films on archaeology (*Tikal*) and ethnography (*Dani Houses* and *Dani Sweet Potatoes*) and is the author of *Ethnographic Film* (1976) and *Indonesian Cinema* (1991).

GAIL MATTHEWS received her Ph.D. in folklore from Indiana University in Bloomington. She holds an adjunct position with the Department of Anthropology at the University of South Carolina and teaches American folklore at South Carolina College. Matthews also serves as a folklore and oral history consultant for arts councils, humanities organizations, and schools. She is currently a delegate to the South Carolina Curriculum Congress and a member of the Arts in Basic Curriculum steering committee.

ANN MESSER is a ninth-grade teacher at South Laurel Junior High School in London, Kentucky. She teaches English and French.

GARY W. MCDONOGH is a professor of anthropology at New College of the University of South Florida. His work has focused on symbolic structures of conflict and the production of culture in urban settings. He is the author of *Good Families of Barcelona: A Social History of Power in the Industrial Era* and *Black and Catholic in Savannah*.

VIRGINIA MOORE is a graduate student at the University of North Carolina at Chapel Hill, working on a Ph.D. in anthropology.

ETHELYN G. ORSO received her Ph.D. in anthropology from Tulane University following her field research in folk medicine in Costa Rica. Her primary interest is in folklore, both regional (Louisiana) and international (European). A former editor of the *Louisiana Folklore Miscellany*, she is a professor of anthropology at the University of New Orleans, where she has taught since 1969. Her publications include *Modern Greek Humor*, *The St. Joseph Altar Traditions of South Louisiana*, and *The Macha of Chira: Confessions of an Anthropologist*.

JAMES PEACOCK is a professor of anthropology at the University of North Carolina at Chapel Hill. He has done extensive fieldwork on theater and religion in Indonesia and the South. Among his publications are *Rites of Modernization*, *Muslim Puritans*, and *Pilgrims of Paradise* (with Ruel W. Tyson). Peacock was drawn to the Confederacy by birth in its capital, Montgomery, Alabama. He rejoined the Union by election to the presidency of the American Anthropological Association in 1991.

Contributors

JOHN EDGAR REID, JR., received his Ph.D. in communication, with a minor in cultural anthropology, from the University of Southern Mississippi. He holds the rank of assistant professor in the Department of Telecommunications at the University of Georgia. He is involved in a number of media-related ethnographic research projects including cross-cultural investigation of Eastern European media systems. His film credits include "Uptown Christian Soldiers," an ethnodocumentary aired on WTTW, Chicago. Currently he is conducting archival research in the George Foster Peabody Collection.

PATSY WEST is director of the Seminole/Miccosukee Photographic Archive, Fort Lauderdale, Florida. A former museum curator, she is an active contributor to the documentation of Seminole/Miccosukee history and preservation of historic sites.

MAX E. WHITE received his B.A. and M.A. degrees in anthropology from the University of Georgia and a Ph.D. in anthropology from Indiana University. He has conducted fieldwork among the Eastern Cherokees, Southern Appalachian mountain people, and rural blacks and has participated in numerous archaeological projects. He currently teaches at Piedmont College, Demorest, Georgia.

CINDY HING-YUK WONG holds an M.A. in visual anthropology from the University of Southern California. She has written, directed, and produced the ethnographic video *Leaving Home: Two Vietnamese Buddhist Lives* and has published on Asian-Americans in the United States. She is currently working on video projects dealing with race, gender, and class in Barcelona.

Index

Abrahams, Roger, 14
Adair, John, 150
African-Americans: as trickster figures in film, 14–16; in genre films, 34–36; as entertainers, 55–73
Altman, Robert, 24–27
Ancelet, Barry, 13
Anderson, Benedict, 113
Anthropology: visual, 1
Appalachia, 77–85, 127–45, 163–89
Appalshop, 4, 127–45
Archaeology: on film, 2
Archive: television, 103–11

Bakhtin, Mikhail, 171
Band of Angels, 32, 33
Baudrillard, Jean, 31
Black Americans. *See* African-Americans
Blank, Les, 13
Boehmer, Edith M., 96–99
Boehmer, William Dyer, 96–99
Brown, James, 64
Burch, Noel, 31, 37
Burns, Ken, 112–23
Butler, Ivan, 42, 43

Campbell, Edward, 31
Capron, Louis, 95
Cash, W. J., 48 (n.3)
Chaney, Lon, 71
Civil War, The: as obsession, 20, 21; on film, 112–23
Civil War, The, 112–23
Combs, James E., 176
Connelly, Thomas, 46
Cool Hand Luke, 42–43

Cory, Charles Barney, 88, 89, 90
Creel, Lorenzo D., 91
Cultural studies, 28

Deliverance, 165
Densmore, Francis, 92
Dimmock, Anthony W., 90, 91
Dimmock, Julian A., 90, 91
Driving Miss Daisy, 29, 41–42

Easy Rider, 13
Edgar, Patricia, 176

Ferris, William, 31
Ferguson, Leland, 2
Film: genres, 9–11; fiction in, 9–23, 24–54, 135, 165, 171–72. *See also* Genre, film
Fisk, John, 176
Flaherty, Robert, 12
Fletch Lives, 11–22
Folklore, 2, 14; Civil War mythologized, 112–23; narrative conventions, 154–56
French, Warren, 31

Gaines, Jane, 4
Gaston, Paul, 46
Genre, film: plantation, 31–43; African-American, 34–36; plainfolk, 36–39
Georgia, 77–85, 103–11
Gone with the Wind, 32–34
Graves, John Temple, 20
Greeley, Andrew, 48 (n.1)
Griffith, D. W., 37

Historians, 1
Horton, Andrew, 12
Hurley, Neil P., 43
Hurricane Hugo, 2, 4, 146–59

Jansen, William Hugh, 16
Jeffords, Susan, 26
Jezebel, 33
Jonestown massacre, 172
Joyner, Charles, 2, 113

Keenan, Kevin, 105
Keith, Don Lee, 9, 10
Kentucky, 127–45
Kirby, Jack, 29, 31
Kiser, Jeff, 130

Langer, John, 175
Legacy of Conflict, 113
Leites, Nathan, 3
Louisiana, 9–23
Louisiana Story, 12, 13

McCullers, Carson, 44
McNeil, William K., 173
Mahabharata, 114, 120
Martin, Jane, 163–64
Mitchell, Margaret, 32
Morales, Beatriz, 2
Motion Picture Production Code, 30
Munroe, Mary Barr, 91
Myth. *See* Folklore

Nashville, 24–28
Newcomb, Horace, 174
Nimmo, Don, 176
North Carolina, 55–73

O'Connell, Neil, 26, 48 (n.1)
O'Conner, Flannery, 45
Oliver, Paul, 64
On Our Own Land, 138–40, 143–44

Painter, Nell, 48 (n.3)
Parks, Arva Moore, 88

People Who Take Up Serpents, The, 190–200
Percy, Walker, 112
Photographs: still, 77–85, 86–102, 114
Pitch a Boogie Woogie, 55–73
Portraits and Dreams, 133–42
Positivism, 4
Postman, Neil, 176
Powdermaker, Hortense, 46

Reagan, Ronald, 47
Religion, 24–53; and television evangelists, 21; absence of, 33; snake handling as, 163–89
Ritchin, Fred, 169
Robinson, Gretchen, 190–200
Rockwood, Caroline Washburn, 87
Romanes, R. A., 77–85

Sanders, Scott, 148
School video projects, 128–45, 146–59
Seltzer, Curtis, 173
Selznick, David O., 32
Seminole: photographs of, 86–102
Sergeant York, 38–39
Skinner, Alanson, 90
Smith, Herb E., 129
Snake handlers, 163–89, 190–200
South, the: definition of, 29, 46–47, 135–36. *See also* stereotypes of
South Carolina, 146–59, 190–200
Spagnolo, Mark, 2
Spitzer, Nicholas, 12
Steel Magnolias, 40–41
Stereotypes of the South, 190–200; speech, 17, 18; sex-hungry women, 18, 19; racism, 19; hospitality, 19, 20; the Civil War obsession, 20, 21; stupidity, 21, 22; food, 22; snake handlers, 163–89
Strangers and Kin, 135–36, 138, 141, 142, 144
Stuart, Andrea, 35, 36

Talking With . . ., 163–66
Television archive, 103–11

Index

They Shall Take Up Serpents, 178–79
Tyson, Ruel, 30

Videotape, 146–59

Walker, Alice, 36
Wallace, Michele, 35, 36
War. *See* Civil War, The; *Sergeant York*
Waters, H. Lee, 2
Welty, Eudora, 84
West, Alex, 2

Whisnant, David, 173
Whiteside, Tom, 2
Wise Blood, 44–45
Wolfenstein, Martha, 3
Woodward, C. Vann, 45
Wooten, Elizabeth, 143–44
Worth, Sol, 150

Yacowar, Maurice, 12, 22, 45, 49 (n.7)
Yoruba in Atlanta, 2